MAGUI BLOCK

HEAL YOUR FAMILY

Get Love and Life to Flow from Your
Ancestors to You and Your Children

BALBOA.
PRESS

A DIVISION OF HAY HOUSE

Balboa Press books may be ordered through booksellers or by contacting:

Balboa Press
A Division of Hay House
1663 Liberty Drive
Bloomington, IN 47403
www.balboapress.com
1 (877) 407-4847

Print information available on the last page.

ISBN: 978-1-5043-9042-2 (sc)
ISBN: 978-1-5043-9041-5 (hc)
ISBN: 978-1-5043-9043-9 (e)

Library of Congress Control Number: 2017916636

Balboa Press rev. date: 01/30/2018

To my children, who compel me to keep finding ways of taking
the best from my ancestors so I can pass it on to them

Contents

Preface

YOU'RE GOING THROUGH LIFE CARRYING heavy baggage full of your invisible family legacy. Unfortunately, you have no idea what it is you've got in there. What's worse is that your children and grandchildren will carry that same baggage. Every member of the family clones that baggage and, further, adds more weight.

Do you believe that in order to heal what you carry from your family legacy you have to go to therapy and review in depth every story from the past with a box of tissues by your side? Many believe that dipping into their family affairs is like opening Pandora's box: there's something very dark in there that will get out of control and generate more suffering than well-being. This is why they resist looking. Others spend years, money, and tears trying to figure out what is happening to them, and still, they end up unsuccessful.

In fact, none of this is necessary. Would you like to know how to liberate yourself and your offspring from your family burden? I will explain how to do that in this book. I will take you by the hand and help you achieve it. I have summarized the essential aspects in a very simple manner, and I share case histories and personal experiences so that you can go through the process with humor and joy.

Using the Magui Block Method, you will lovingly transform what you find heavy about your family so that the only thing that comes to you from your family is what drives you toward life, achieving your greatest potential. Whether you have taken personal growth courses before or are a beginner, this book was written with you in mind. Using the knowledge I have acquired through more than twenty-five years of experience as a psychotherapist, I have combined the most advanced and powerful techniques into the Magui Block Method so that you can enjoy the benefits immediately.

My approach contradicts conventional thinking and proclaims that liberating family burdens can be quick, easy and fun. Sound too good to be true? Here are testimonials given by students of this method after taking one of my seminars:

- "The Magui Block Method is practical, quick, and effective."

- "It works marvelously and magically."

- "Magui made it so easy!"

- "I loved her passion, respect, and love, and of course her joy. I leave here pleasantly surprised as a result of all the tools I was given. I recommend this to everyone on the road to awakening."

- "I dropped 27 kilograms by using the method and without expecting to."

- "It's a marvelous and wise method, and I found Magui's love, joy, and devotion, her knowledge and experience extraordinary."

- "I love this method because it goes in so deep, in such a clear manner, and I get effective results that make me very happy."

- "I find this method absolutely marvelous!"

- "I enjoyed acquiring new tools through humor and light."

- "I'm new at this and seeing how you get to the root of the problem and find the solution so quickly is surprising to me."

- "I leave here feeling happy, relaxed after having liberated myself from many things that were bothering me and that I was unaware of."

- "The Magui Block Method has a level of impeccability and clarity that is profoundly transformative, and the most important thing is that it is empowering."

- "I love the Magui Block Method because it's very powerful and complete."

- "I noticed many aspects that were keeping me stuck, and I now have the tools with which to resolve them."

- "It's a method that lovingly points out your flaws, and just as lovingly they are healed, and you're well-ordered again."

- "I'm forever surprised at how profound the transformation is."

In this book, I share the way in which family systems work because it's common to get caught up in their destructive dynamics. I also share how to create order and harmony so that the energy of life flows from your ancestors to you and then gets shared with your offspring. I'm gathering all the resources at my disposal and sharing them with you by writing this book because I have a very ambitious objective: to heal your family.

This book is written in a special way, so that your conscious mind concentrates on theoretical topics while your unconscious mind focuses on your healing. This occurs through the combination of techniques that I use throughout the book together with your intention to heal your family and my intention to help you achieve it. All this comes about because of the many years of training and professional experience I have had, for which I am very grateful. The transformation will happen like magic.

The techniques I use include knowledge gained from several teachers with whom I've had the privilege of training. Indeed, everything I offer has come to me from others. I have merely merged the techniques with my personal style, combining them in my preferred way.

Given that there are techniques that are so loving and easy to use, I find it sad that there are families in which every generation repeats the same stories, growing increasingly heavy and painful. Invisible family legacies are like snowballs; they get bigger as they roll along. That's why I consider it urgent that this material comes to light so that many people benefit from it. Start with yourself, and you'll heal your family. Let's begin!

Introduction

WHAT DOES IT MEAN TO "heal your family"? Does it refer to healing the members of your family, or you relative to your family? Is it about healing others—your whole family—or healing yourself?

You are part of your family. You're a member of the family, and as such, you belong to it. This is clear and does not require any explanation. What does require an explanation is why your family is a part of *you*.

You are much more than you realize, and an important part of you is your family. Your family is a part of you in your history and the information that was passed on to you at the moment you were conceived. You began living in your body the moment your mother's egg and your father's sperm were united. The family information was contained in these seeds—from the shape of your body to the way you think. These seeds not only gave you life but also provided you with the basic information you need to survive and function. They pass on all the rules of the game that served your ancestors in the past.

Many people still have doubts about this. They believe they inherit physical traits—such as the color of their skin or the size of their eyes—but not their way of being and of functioning in the world. They consider these things to be entirely independent of the family. However, in working with people who were raised by adoptive families since childbirth, I have observed traits in their manner of thinking and behaving that are related to their biological family. How is that possible if there has never been any contact between them?

What is the connection between children and their biological parents if they were raised by adoptive parents? Why do they end up being like their biological family in their habits? Why does everything that happens and everything that happened in your family of origin affect you so much? Because all family members are connected by an invisible bond. All share the same heritage and participate in it by taking and giving information.

I call this heritage the *invisible family legacy*. All incidents, important and not so important, are stored in it, including the story of each family member and that individual's beliefs and emotions. It's like a gigantic file you've accessed and downloaded just by being a member of the family. The problem is that you downloaded a lot of information that is disadvantageous, and so your memory is full of how you've been hurt. There's no space left to store what is nourishing.

To heal your family is to clean out from your individual memory bank the family information that is harmful to you and leave only what is beneficial to you. It involves acknowledging that something in your family legacy is affecting you negatively, and understanding that you can modify that information within you. By changing it inside you, you change it for the entire family because you add a new updated version to the family databank. All members of the family will now have access to it.

Imagine a family in which the common thread is to be overweight. The babies are born large, and everything contributes to weight gain, from eating and life habits to way of thinking. All of a sudden, one of the members modifies that way of thinking, exercises, eats healthily, and reaches an ideal weight. This new information enters the family legacy, and now there are two possibilities for this family—being overweight or having the ideal weight—when before only the overweight option existed.

The goal of this book, *Heal Your Family,* is to move you toward healing relative to what is happening and has happened in your family. Your actions will have an immediate impact on your entire family because you are a part of it and it is a part of you. One cannot move without the other. At the same time, each member of the family, within the available options, can choose what he or she desires. Respecting what every person desires is essential to healing.

The first step is wanting to move toward healing. If you want another member of the family to move first, which often seems logical, all your attention will be focused on changing that individual. But you only have power over yourself. When you change, you will be changing the family indirectly. That in turn will influence the other family member to change if he or she chooses to.

Focus on learning and modifying your own part. Remember, you are your family, and your family is you. When you change yourself, your family changes, and all its members have new positive possibilities available to them within their inheritance. For example, if depression runs in your family, by healing that aspect within you, you integrate that solution into the family legacy. It's so much easier than getting a depressed person to read this book and apply its teachings.

This is how it works for everything else. Heal yourself of all those aspects that are a worry to those you love, and in doing so, you will modify the invisible family legacy. As a result, your loved ones will have better possibilities.

I recommend that as you read this book, you concentrate on yourself and on what is happening to you relative to your family. People are surprised by the changes they observe in their family members, and it's hard for them to recognize that the changes started with them. Change yourself, and you will change your family. I assure you—I've witnessed this time and again.

Chapter 1

The Magui Block Method for Healing Your Family

F ROM AS EARLY AS I can remember, I've had a special way of perceiving what goes on around me. Even as a young child, I was passionate about the dynamics between people, and I used to invent entanglements and then find different solutions for them. I had very well-developed empathy. I could feel in my body what other people were feeling and see the images they created in their minds. This caused a lot of confusion about what belonged to me and what belonged to others.

I didn't know how to handle what some people called *gifts*; I experienced them as curses. When it came time to choose a profession, I had no idea what to do. I ended up getting a bachelor's degree in administration and worked as an administrator and consultant for seven years. With a steady job that provided me with structure and a sensation of being normal in the world, I began applying my particular powers in service to others without fully realizing what I was doing.

While I worked as an administrative director at a school, I studied psychotherapy and offered some private consultations. Psychotherapy was my hobby—something I did for the pleasure of learning. While I studied different psychotherapeutic techniques, I also learned to use my gifts with people at work. I was increasingly motivated by the transformations I saw and marveled at how easy the process could be when using the correct technique. I continued to train with the best teachers and to find new formulae for creating rapid changes.

By then, I was married and had two beautiful children. I applied everything I learned to myself and my family. I can say that I had the perfect family for practicing on what I was studying. Over the next few years, I went through extremely difficult situations involving myself and those I loved: health problems, hospitalizations, emergency operations, serious and chronic illnesses, deaths, depression, losing a job, even violent situations like robberies and assaults. Conflicts appeared in all areas of my life—health, family, friends, profession, finances, and relationships—so I had the chance to apply what I was studying to the problems in my own life. I experimented and developed my own way of settling conflicts. I combined techniques and created new ones.

People began to seek me out to work with them, but I had neither a consulting room nor any interest in giving consultations. At that time, I considered myself an administrator by profession and would refer them to my teachers, but with the increase in calls, I understood what my true vocation was: to transform through love. As soon as I said yes to psychotherapy as a profession and set up a consulting room, my life changed dramatically.

My consultations multiplied. I had a waiting list that went out for several months. I was invited to create materials for training the facilitators of the Institute of Resonance Repatterning. With such high demand for consultations, I thought it was an excellent idea to train more students, so in turn more people could be treated.

My life transformed rapidly. I became a writer of training manuals and a teacher of seminars, and I traveled the world. I have had the opportunity to get to know Canada, South Africa, Chile, Argentina, Spain, the United Kingdom, and many places in the United States and Mexico. Since many people asked to be trained but had no previous experience with the material, I decided to create the Magui Block Method for anyone who has experienced the need for a change and simply knows how to read and write. I wrote new training manuals and created two diploma programs to prepare facilitators in the method.

I gave conferences and workshops for over fifteen years, and I was asked many times to write a book. I did have manuals, but they were only available to people who were training to be facilitators. What about all those people who only wanted to heal themselves? Why did they have to invest so much time and money in learning? Still, I had enormous resistance to writing a book. I felt it could lead to huge changes for me. Nothing would be the same again. This was not logical thinking; it was based only on a sensation.

As I write this now, I can feel that sensation of a new beginning. I've made up my mind that this book needs to be written to transform lives. If only one person benefits, I will be satisfied. I hope that person is you!

What Is the Magui Block Method and How Does It Work?

The Magui Block Method combines the most advanced techniques in psychotherapy in a unique way to get effective results in an extraordinarily short time. Although I take elements and ideas from many teachers, the main support for this book comes from the theories established by Bert Hellinger, the creator of Family Constellations. I also include knowledge from other schools, trainings, and techniques and from my own personal experience, as well as the experiences of my clients. The influences I want to mention are:

- Family Constellations
- Resonance Repatterning
- Ericksonian hypnosis
- Gestalt psychotherapy
- Person-centered focus
- ZhiNeng QiGong
- Emotional Freedom Technique (EFT)
- Tapas Acupressure Technique (TAT)
- Eye Movement Desensitization and Reprocessing (EMDR)

As I continually create new ways of resolving client/family conflict, the method continues to grow and evolve, but what has stood the test of time is how it works. I can summarize it in the following three movements that occur when you achieve positive change:

1. You identify the entanglement, the negative aspects, the problem—whatever it is that keeps you trapped in a situation of conflict.
2. You identify the resource—what you need instead of the conflict. In other words, the solution.
3. You transform yourself. This is where the magic lies! When you put all the pieces together, a change occurs—a leap if you will—and you find yourself in a new place where the problem seems very distant and small.

During the practice, each of these movements can take place through various smaller movements, in a different order, or they can be combined in one unified movement. The important thing is for you to transform, and you do that by acknowledging your problem and integrating the resources that are missing. There are many ways of achieving this, but I like that it happens through love and, if possible, a dash of humor as well.

Throughout the book, I use a range of diverse examples to help you better understand the method. Though the examples are real, I have changed the names of the people involved to protect their privacy.

What Can the Magui Block Method Do for You and Your Family?

To date, I have used my method in my private practice; in the conferences and workshops I give; and as I train facilitators—all to great success. Through this book, I am sharing my method with the public at large using the method to get the same results. I have written this book so that you can embody the three movements of healing—identifying your entanglements and problems, obtaining resources, and transforming yourself—without even realizing how it's happening. You'll be transforming yourself as if by magic.

Your conscious mind will focus on what I'm explaining to you while your unconscious mind activates your healing forces. Your left hemisphere will understand the theoretical concepts, and your right hemisphere will create images acknowledging the chaos and then substitute with images of order and harmony. Your internal images or pictures are movies you create in your mind, and they have incredible power to heal. All this occurs as you read in comfort.

Your mind and your emotions have an effect on your body. Your body also has an effect on your mind and your emotions. While you are reading, at times I'll ask you to adopt a specific body posture, evoke love, and state a declaration out loud. By following these requests, you open up certain points and conduits of energy in your body. Your mind expands, and you're prepared to integrate positive change. I learned these postures in my ZhiNeng QiGong practice.

You evoke love as the highest element to function as a catalyst, thereby making this a gentle process. By stating out loud that which synthesizes the issue to be resolved, you are affirming your decision to change. It's like saying "I do" when you get married. Everyone would suppose that if you've shown up at the church, dressed for the occasion, it's because you want to be married. But still you are asked, right? That "I do" is very important because it refers to your free will and gives you the power to choose. By stating the declaration out loud—taking on the body posture as I describe it—you're mobilizing your power of transformation. Actively following along with what I will be suggesting to you, you'll achieve extraordinary changes, and it only takes a few minutes.

Something that blocks transformation is your specific intention for members of the family. What do I mean by this? I'm referring to your desires or expectations regarding other family members, for example, for the son to be married, for the partner to get a job, for the mother to be loving, for the father to drop his addiction. It might be that intentions like these are what led you to read this book, but in order to accomplish this change, you need to set them aside and concentrate on the part you have to play. Forget about what's bothering you about others for a while. It will be like when you have an issue you can't resolve and you go to the movies to get your mind off things, and on the way home the solution comes to you. This is what you are going to do. Set your intention to one side and concentrate on the bigger goal: healing your family by healing yourself.

You'll be surprised by how easily and quickly this can happen. On occasion, you'll only note changes occurring in you. Sometimes you'll notice changes in others. Overall, you will enjoy the transformations in yourself and the other members of your family. For some people, these changes come immediately; others take a few months to see them. Each person integrates things in his or her own rhythm because the intention is for this process to be loving, crisis-free, quick, yet soft and joyful. Place your attention on your reading and on doing what I tell you to do with the overall intention of healing your family by healing yourself, and let go of specific intentions. Are you ready?

Chapter 2

The Invisible Family Legacy

E VERY HUMAN BEING IS UNIQUE and unrepeatable, but we all have something in common: we are conceived by a father and a mother. As soon as the mother's egg and the father's sperm come together, you receive your invisible family legacy. Regardless of what happens later—how you are raised, the relationship you have with your parents, or your traumas in infancy—you receive a legacy when you are conceived, and this affects you profoundly.

Often when you seek out the root of a problem, the tendency is to give most importance to what occurred in early infancy and the way you were raised. The idea being to find solutions in relationships with important authority figures from the past—the first ones on that list being your mother and your father, generally in that order. However, I assure you that many of the personal problems you have not yet resolved have their origin in your invisible family legacy and not in what happened in your childhood. My professional experience has shown me that most of my clients' problems have their source in what they are carrying from their family. That is why, on recognizing their legacy and taking advantage of it, they achieve extraordinary changes and transformations they were previously unable to achieve even after years of traditional therapy.

Your invisible family legacy is everything you receive at the moment of your conception. It is the information that comes in your mother's egg and your father's sperm. It includes information you received at the unconscious level from your family. This information is not only what occurred in the past, it's what keeps happening in the present. As long as members of a family are alive, the family system shifts and reorganizes, the information changes, and there are updates that affect all parties, positively and negatively.

That's why this invisible family legacy is in perpetual change—you and all members of the family system have access to it, and every one of you can make changes. You can be controlled by it, as happens to most people, or you can take your power and learn to use this information to your greatest advantage. You just need to learn how to do this, and this book will teach you.

Contained within your invisible family legacy are emotions, beliefs, stories, loyalties, and traumas. People tend to forget these subtle aspects; however, many times that is where the root of the problem lies, and therefore the solution as well. The invisible family legacy can be a very heavy load to carry for both you and your offspring. Let me share some examples of how it might be affecting your lives:

- Financial problems might have their origin in a loss of goods or money on the part of one of your ancestors.

- You may feel unhappy, depressed, or grumpy because you are carrying emotions that belong to another family member.

- An inability to get what you want—or getting it and then losing it—might be due to a family loyalty.

- Problems with reestablishing a healthy and happy relationship with your mate might arise because you are repeating the story of other family members.

- Fears, anxieties, insomnia, or acts of violence might be caused by a trauma someone in your family experienced.

- Having accidents, being assaulted, or finding yourself in any situation where your life is in danger could occur because you are unconsciously repeating ancestral cycles of violence.

- Any destructive habit could come about as a result of tragic deaths suffered in the family.

It's easy to understand that what happens in your family affects you when you get to know your biological family and relate to it. What is really hard to understand for most people, is how something they're not even aware of, can affect them. How is it possible that the story of some ancestor they have never met, like a great grandmother, is the cause of their child's depression? Or how can the emotions of someone you don't believe belonged to the family, such as your maternal grandfather's lover, be the cause of your not being able to consolidate a healthy relationship with your spouse?

The answer is that this information is stored in your family legacy, and since it's invisible, it affects you without your being aware of it. It's as if you were a puppet being toyed with by the stories of many members of your family. You think you hold your own strings, but that is not the case. You think you are free, but you're trapped.

The first step in moving ahead in your process is to acknowledge that you are carrying this legacy. Envision a small woman with a large bag on her shoulder that contains things she has been accumulating without realizing it. If she continues to deny that the bag is too big for her bone structure, she's going to walk through life all askew because of the weight. On the other hand, if she acknowledges it, she'll be willing to stop, open the bag, and empty the contents to look at what serves her and what she needs to let go of.

In order to take the next step, you need to acknowledge you have a family legacy and that it weighs on you more heavily than you had thought. At the same time, you still don't know specifically what this legacy contains or in what ways it's affecting you. For now, merely open up to the possibility that some of the problems you have been having and have not resolved are coming from that place.

My objective with this book is ambitious. Not only will it teach you the theory of the Magui Block Method, but by reading it you can transform yourself easily and lovingly. I've put in one part by explaining the method, and you put in the other by applying the method. In adopting the right posture, evoking love, and repeating the phrase I propose out loud, you are going to weave together your body, mind, and emotions to create a loving transformation.

First, adopt the right physical posture, as follows:

- Hold your body upright. Imagine that your head is touching the sky and that your feet are firmly and deeply grounded in the earth.

- Be centered. Your heart and mind are as clear as crystal.

- Place your hands, one over the other, on your belly button. Imagine that they connect to the space that is close to your spine, inside of your body. (If you're a woman, place the palm of your right hand on your belly button and the palm of the left hand on the back of your right hand. If you're a man, place the palm of your left hand on your belly button and the palm of the right hand on the back of your left hand.)

Next, evoke love:

- Remember your willingness to heal, and smile.
- Feel appreciation for yourself.
- Be thankful for the moment.

Finally, appreciate the power of these words :

- Repeat these phrases out loud.
- Listen to the way you say them, and repeat them until they come naturally to you.

Now, adopt the right posture, evoke love, and repeat the following out loud:

> *I acknowledge that I am carrying an invisible family legacy and that this is affecting me. I now choose to get to know my family legacy and transform it through love.*

How to Obtain the Greatest Benefit from Your Family Legacy

Your inheritance is given when you are born into the family you belong to. You do not choose what you receive, but you can modify it once you've recognized it and get the most out of it. In general, when one receives something nice, the sentiment is one of gratitude, but when it's unpleasant, rejection and contempt arise.

The same thing happens in your family. If your family pleases you, you're going to appreciate your legacy. If your family—or certain members or aspects of it—are not to your liking, you'll feel like rejecting it. What you most reject is strengthened; that is to say, it gets bigger and weighs even more heavily.

Imagine that your family is like a university. You arrived at this specific university to acquire certain basic schooling. You can do whatever you like with this, from moaning about your teachers, the institution, and your schoolmates to taking advantage of the gym, taking extra classes, taking too many courses, doing your homework, and studying for exams. You can go to private consultations with the teachers who are the best at explaining things; you can party every night; you can get together with the brainy ones in the group or those who are good at sports. What would you like your experience to be like?

Your siblings are at the same university, but do they do the same things as you? Of course not! Every person chooses a different experience according to what he or she can and wishes to do.

I believe you are born into the right family for you—the one that has the legacy that corresponds to you in this life, with the learning and experiences you want to have. Working with thousands of people, I've realized that when the family legacy is very heavy, a greater possibility for growth becomes evident, as long as you adopt the right attitude. If you think about the university, one big family load is equivalent to studying several professional careers at the same time. This means many hours of study, but it's worth it in the end.

The key lies in your attitude toward your family. "Poor me! What did I do to deserve this family? It's not fair!" is an attitude that places you in a situation of being the victim. These thoughts get in the way of facing what you're experiencing and getting the most out of your legacy. On the other hand, when you concentrate on what corresponds to you in your family, you only take on your small part, and you liberate yourself from all the rest. This fills you up with power. In giving back to each person his or her responsibility, you can then take advantage of your legacy.

Consider the story of Erika, the eldest of three sisters. Ever since she was little, she was treated like the male child her father was hoping for. More was demanded of her, and less was given to her. Her greatest longing was to be a mother, but she had not been able to consolidate a stable couple relationship, and she had lost two babies during the first months of pregnancy.

Erika came to my consulting room and could not stop crying. She felt frustrated and sad because her father had just bought her middle sister an apartment and had sent her youngest sister on a luxury trip to Europe, while at the same time he owed Erika money that she desperately needed. She thought this was all very unfair and felt wretched.

Is this situation unfair for Erika? Of course it is. But she cannot change what her father does. That is his affair, and he is the only one who can do anything about it. Erika can only work on her own part. What part is that? She is unconsciously trying to please her father and be the son he wanted but never had. No matter what she does, she cannot be his son, and she is unconsciously ruling out her desire to have children. In carrying her father's expectations, she is unconsciously giving up on her dream.

If she can get out of victim mode—where she is resentful of her father for being unfair—and stop paying attention to what her sisters are getting from their father and feeling sorry for herself, she'll also stop lending him money, especially when she needs it and he just gives it away. She'll then be fully empowered and able to take on the role of older sister. She will allow her father to face the consequences of all his wrongs, and she will be thankful for what she has.

Changing your attitude and leaving behind the position of victim leads you to find the lessons in your family experience. When you learn what you need to learn, you take the right actions and get yourself out of destructive dynamics. If you continue down the road of being the victim, on the other hand, you will keep repeating the same painful story. Everything starts with the simplest of steps: changing your attitude, even if your story is still the same, without washing over what is happening and without looking at it through rose-tinted glasses. If it's unfair, that's the way it is. Stop trying to change it when it's not in your power to do so. Shift what is under your control.

A change in attitude is a choice you make. You choose the attitude you take vis-à-vis what you experience. Unless there is a mental or emotional illness that prevents this—because you've sunk into a deep depression or have been otherwise weakened—you have the power to change your attitude by modifying your thoughts. Stop thinking your situation is unfair or wrong, and remember your family is your university. Realize you are carrying an overload of subjects when something you're facing is painful. Do what it takes to carry only your own part of the burden.

Further down the line, I'm going to provide you with ways to recognize and carry your part only. For the moment, concentrate on adopting the right attitude—the one you find empowering. When your thinking is, "Poor me, what I'm experiencing is unfair," you feel like a victim of circumstance and believe you have no power to face what is going on. When your thinking is, "What happens to me in my family is an opportunity for me to become a better person," you fill up with power and resources.

So now, on to using the Magui Block Method. Adopt the right physical posture as follows:

- Hold your body upright. Imagine that your head is touching the sky and that your feet are firmly and deeply grounded in the earth.

- Be centered. Your heart and mind are as clear as crystal.

- Place your hands, one over the other, on your belly button. Imagine that they connect to the space that is close to your spine, inside of your body. (If you're a woman, place the palm of your right hand on your belly button and the palm of the left hand on the back of your right hand. If you're a man, place the palm of your left hand on your belly button and the palm of the right hand on the back of your left hand.)

Next, evoke love:

- Remember your willingness to heal, and smile.
- Feel appreciation for yourself.
- Be thankful for the moment.

Finally, appreciate the power of these words :

- Repeat these phrases out loud.
- Listen to the way you say them, and repeat them until they come naturally to you.

Now, adopt the right posture, evoke love, and repeat the following out loud:

> *I recognize my attitude of victimhood and transform it.*
> *I now choose to empower myself and learn my lesson in the situation I'm experiencing.*

If you find yourself in some family situation that you don't like and don't understand why you're experiencing it, use the following statements:

> *I recognize my attitude of victimhood and transform it.*
> *I now choose to learn my lesson relative to [name the person or situation you're having trouble with].*

For example, if you're fighting with a former spouse over how to raise your children, the statements would be:

*I recognize my attitude of victimhood and transform it. I
now choose to empower myself and learn my lesson about
how I relate to my former spouse. I find the way to raise
our children with love and wisdom.*

With these statements, you focus on your power, on removing your
attention from what the other is doing, and on the objective of being a
better human being and raising your offspring wisely.

How to Pass Only the Best on to Your Progeny

You and your offspring are repeating family stories without realizing it.
Why do you do that? Out of blind love. In order to pass the best legacy
on to your offspring, you need to teach them to love wisely instead of
blindly. You can only teach what you master, so you're going to begin
by identifying how you love in order to eliminate blind love from your
repertoire. The following cases are going to help you understand how
blind love works.

Whether or not you have a teenage child, envision the following
situation: Your teenager comes home from school sad and withdrawn.
There's a party on Friday that all his schoolmates are invited to except
for him. Every day of this week has been torture for him, and as the date
of the party approaches, your child feels worse. You're suffering through
this together with him. You already have some social activities planned
for this weekend, but you're now feeling split. You don't know whether to
cancel those plans, include your son in the plans, or carry on as if nothing
were happening. You feel guilty about having a good time while your son
is having such a hard time. If you could, you'd change the situation your
child is in so that he could enjoy having a good time with friends who love
him and invite him to parties. You wish you could spare him this pain.

Now, use your imagination to get into the following experience,
whether or not you have a sister: Your little sister has just been the victim
of a fraud. A rogue lied to her, got her to fall in love with him, and then
stole from her. She, in her innocence, lost money, got into trouble with
the law, and is distraught. She no longer trusts love, has legal problems,

and is depressed. You're angry and want to find a way to punish that jerk. You might even feel like beating him up. Sometimes, you dream he's in prison paying for his behavior.

Next, envision that you are in a couple relationship and the following happens: Your partner has a terminal illness and is in the hospital. Because of the institution's regulations, you can only be there for two hours a day. Although the rest of your time you are on your own, all your attention is focused on what you suppose is happening there. You worry about the care your partner is receiving and wish you could be by your loved one's side. You cannot concentrate on anything else. When your partner is given treatments, it hurts as if they were being applied to you. Sometimes you fantasize about switching things around so that you are the one dying in the hospital and your partner is the healthy one.

You can identify with every one of these cases, can't you? In most families, suffering from what someone you love is suffering through is considered a good quality—proof that you have a generous heart. But this manner of loving is precisely what blind love is: a feeling that connects you to the members of the family and gets you to carry something that really belongs to the one you love.

In the first example, blind love makes you carry your son's pain from not being invited to the party. In the second example, blind love gets you to carry the repressed anger in your sister and the need to defend her and have justice be served. In the third example, blind love leads you to get sick and die. None of these issues belongs to you; they belong to a hypothetical family, created to help you learn how blind love works.

It's an illusion to think you can carry other people's burdens and spare them their pain. What really happens is that the pain gets multiplied. Your loved one suffers through what he or she is experiencing, and so do you. Carrying someone else's burden, even in the name of love and with the intention of helping, has many consequences. I'll mention a few:

- *It's disempowering.* When you carry what belongs to someone else, the message you send is: "You can't do this. It's too heavy for you. Let me help you." You show your loved ones with your concern that what they're living through is too much for them and that you can do a better job of carrying their burden. This makes them feel weak because they end up needing you. You're lording it over them, as if you were more capable and strong because you believe you can do it and they cannot. In other words, you carry their burden, because they are incapable of doing it on their own.

- *It repeats the same mistake.* A mistake stops repeating itself when your response to the situation is different. This only happens when you change; and in order to change, you need to learn. The same thing happens to your loved ones. They can learn by experiencing and solving problems, even though it might hurt. Pain teaches lessons.

- *It creates disorder.* There is love and harmony in a well-ordered family. One of the characteristics of order is that all family members carry their own load. Carrying what belongs to another involves letting go of one's own stuff. The problem is that people tend to feel invincible—above all when it comes to saving those they love—so they believe they are capable of carrying the other's load without dropping their own. They believe they can do it all, but every time they carry someone else's package, they let go of their own without realizing it. Others feel obligated to pick it up, in turn letting go of their own load. As you can see, it creates a big mess. Nobody can resolve things for another. The issues just stick around, growing like balloons that are so full of air that they are ready to explode.

To give you an idea of the gravity of the problem, imagine that you're traveling in a group, and you hire a tour company. One of the directions they give you is that you can have just one suitcase—one that you are capable of carrying—and it has to have your name tag on it. Every member of the tour has to take one tagged suitcase of the size he or she can carry.

You set off on your journey, and some people start moving more slowly. They stop to buy souvenirs, fill up their suitcase, and buy new ones. Soon several in the group have more than one suitcase each. Other members offer to carry the additional baggage, all with the best of intentions, which is to get the tour to move more swiftly and have the trip be enjoyable.

The problem is that the suitcases get mixed up. Some of the suitcases have no name tags, nobody knows what belongs to whom, and everyone has to pay for the additional overweight fees on the flights. The worst part is that people keep buying souvenirs and new suitcases because they are not facing the consequences of their actions. So now there are more and more suitcases in the group, nobody knows which is whose, and some carry too much while others keep creating more weight for the rest. Everyone participates in creating chaos and disorder. The journey becomes a nightmare.

- *It multiplies suffering.* Although it might seem that you're lightening the load for someone you love, you are in fact multiplying it. A common occurrence when a member of the family has to be hospitalized is for the entire family to go along, taking turns sitting vigil. They all wait around for hours, sitting or standing, no sleeping, no eating, because they believe this is how to love—by suffering together through the one family member's disaster.

Another example is when your spouse or your mother gets sick, and you get sick along with her, so now you both feel awful. How does this spare her any discomfort? Yet your subconscious tells you that it's right to suffer along with the person you love. Being happy while the other suffers is considered treason. If you only knew that in suffering along with the person you love, you're creating more suffering, you'd stop this behavior. But this is where another element comes in: guilt. This guilt comes from feeling fine while the other is feeling bad and is the topic of a different chapter. For now, realize you are multiplying the suffering when you take on others' pain and you spare them nothing.

- *It replicates tragic stories.* When some members of the family suffer through a tragic story, other members repeat the story through blind love. For example, a grandfather loses his goods and his money. This depresses him, and he dies soon thereafter, poor, with all illusions shattered. The grandmother focuses on working hard so as to make sure her children get ahead. Her only joy is for them to be in good financial shape.

The family progeny have many possible tragic stories to replicate. Some will repeat the grandfather's story by being unable to generate the abundance they desire or by diving into depression and disillusionment. Others will replicate the grandmother's pattern, devoting themselves to their offspring and forfeiting any life of their own, or working to excess. Others still will create a combination, such as working to excess and being poor.

Every time a story gets replicated, it is reaffirmed. It's like the channels that water forms on the earth. The more water flows, the deeper the channel runs, and the more water is pulled in that direction. In a similar manner, as more and more people in the family experience a story and, the more it gets reaffirmed, the more likely it is that others will suffer through something similar.

That is why there are families in which several members live alone, have no children, or have financial problems. If you're living out this story of your own free will, that is perfect; the problem is when you want something different but cannot accomplish it because you're unwittingly trapped in a family story—and, to make matters worse, you're transferring it on to your offspring!

Through blind love, you attempt to carry what is causing pain for your loved ones so as to spare them suffering, but in reality, you're harming them when what you most desire is to give them the very best.

All family members need to carry the load that corresponds to them. There are many reasons for this. Here are a few:

- *To learn a lesson.* Although we might not understand it, sometimes a person needs to go down a painful road or one of suffering in order to pick up certain lessons. If you carry other people's pain, you might prevent them from suffering now, but if they need the specific experience, sooner or later, they'll have it. You may wish they did not have to experience it at all, but if that were true, then why are they having that experience? They need to experience what is happening, suffer through it, and resolve it.

You can support them in the practical aspects of life. If we continue with the previous examples, you could take your sister to see a good lawyer or talk to your son and create possible strategies for improving his social life. In the case of your spouse, you might seek out the best possible medical treatment. Supporting your loved ones this way, by looking for solutions, is vastly different from carrying their pain.

- *To become empowered.* When people confront the situations that life serves up to them, at every turn feeling what is happening, they become stronger and more empowered. On the other hand, when they turn away from what they are living, they connect to their weakness and make themselves small. You allow your loved ones to become empowered when you allow them to take on the responsibility for their load, and you disempower them when you carry what belongs to them.

- *To receive recognition and respect.* If you look at someone who is going through a hard time while keeping an internal state of serenity, the message you send is, "I respect you and acknowledge your value. You can do this."

By loving blindly, you carry the load of others with the idea of sparing them pain, but you merely increase it. By loving them wisely, you allow each one to assume his or her part, and you give your offspring the best legacy. Blind love disappears when it becomes wise.

How to Transform Love from Blind to Wise

These are the steps to transforming blind love to wise love:

1. Feel the love you have for the person.
2. Identify the baggage that belongs to the one you love and acknowledge that it is not for you to carry.
3. Identify your own baggage, the piece that has your name on it, and pick it up.

Envision again the example of being on a tour. All members of the group have their own suitcase with their name tag on it. Read the tags on the suitcases. Each one identifies its owner. The baggage arrives and is on the carousel at the airport. You have to identify your own suitcase and carry it. Acknowledge your loved ones' luggage and let them carry their own bags. Remember, if you carry it for them, they're just going to buy new ones, so it's not such a good idea. Right?

One of the toughest things in life is to watch your child suffering. It's the natural order of things for parents to die before their offspring. That's why, when a child gets sick and the parents are healthy, they yearn to take the child's place and get sick instead. The most painful thing that can befall a father or a mother is to be unable to do anything for a suffering child. In cases like these, how can a parent transform blind love into wise love?

The first step for parents is to acknowledge the love they have for the child and feel how their heart expands with that deep love. The second step is to identify their child's baggage and acknowledge they cannot carry it for the child. The baggage in this case would be the illness. The third and last step is for the parents to identify their own baggage and carry it. Having a sick child is quite a heavy load to carry. Parents want a healthy child who is able to play and do the things that healthy children do. Their luggage is what they are experiencing individually.

If you learn to love wisely, your children will love in like manner. By respecting the stories of each of your family members, you will no longer need to repeat those stories. The suffering ends, and you can give your offspring the best of the family legacy.

You're now going to use the Magui Block Method to pass on to your progeny the best of your family legacy. Adopt the right physical posture:

- Hold your body upright. Imagine that your head is touching the sky and that your feet are firmly and deeply grounded in the earth.

- Be centered. Your heart and mind are as clear as crystal.

- Place your hands, one over the other, on your belly button. Imagine that they connect to the space that is close to your spine, inside of your body. (If you're a woman, place the palm of your right hand on your belly button and the palm of the left hand on the back of your right hand. If you're a man, place the palm of your left hand on your belly button and the palm of the right hand on the back of your left hand.)

Next, evoke love:

- Remember your willingness to heal, and smile.

- Feel appreciation for yourself.

- Be thankful for the moment.

Finally, appreciate the power of these words :

- Repeat these phrases out loud.

- Listen to the way you say them, and repeat them until they come naturally to you.

Now, adopt the right posture, evoke love, and repeat the following out loud:

I learn to love wisely.
I recognize I can only carry my part.
I allow every member of my family to carry his or her load, even if it's painful.
I give my offspring the best legacy by showing them how to carry their own load and stop carrying those of other family members.
All of us carry our own stuff, in our power and in line with our capacity.
I love wisely.
I only carry my own part.
I love wisely.
I allow all family members to carry what belongs to them.
I love wisely.
And I give my offspring the best legacy.

Chapter 3

The Five Keys to Healing Your Family

THERE ARE MANY WAYS TO heal a family, and I've devoted myself to finding the simplest manner to achieve this healing. In the process, I've discovered five keys. These keys are the master keys of family systems. By using them, you'll be able to open any lock that is preventing you from finding the solution to what is ailing you and your loved ones. The five keys are:

1. *Include everyone.*
2. *Get your family in order.*
3. *Take life energy from your ancestors.*
4. *Strike a balance between what you give and what you take.*
5. *Resolve your cycles of violence and find peace.*

Are you ready to learn about each of these keys?

Key #1: Include Everyone

Just as there are laws in the judicial system for regulating legacies, there are laws in family systems. The family laws are the law of the complete number and the law of the right to belong. *The law of the complete number* specifies that only when all members of the family system are included and have a dignified place will there be peace and a feeling of being complete. *The law of the right to belong* states that any member of the family, regardless of what he or she is like, has the same right to belong as any of the others. That is to say, all members of the family system belong to the family.

To explain these two laws, let's go back of the tour group. Imagine that you have been traveling for six months through inhospitable countries with a group of people you just met at the beginning of this trip. Over the months, you have spent time together on airplanes, buses, and historic tours. You've had to get up really early, gone without a shower, traveled while tired, and been in every possible mood. You belong to the same tour. You are part of a system.

If, on some part of the journey, one of the tourists does not arrive in time to board the bus, the entire group will certainly feel a degree of anxiety. The sensation is, "Someone's missing." This sensation exists because of the law of the complete number. Every time a system is formed—that is to say, a group of people with a similar intention or of a specific quality—the laws kick in. The sensation of discomfort and of being incomplete is much stronger when the person missing is a family member.

Now imagine there's someone on the tour many of the others don't like because this person is different. Some would love for that person to be taken off the tour because they believe this individual disturbs the harmony in the group. However, this person has the same right to belong as the others and must be given a dignified place—that is, be respected and treated as an equal. If this member is not treated respectfully by the others, even though this might not be shown openly, the entire system suffers.

Now, imagine that this person is the one who has not made it to the bus on time. Apparently, several members of the tour are happy about this and think that finally they'll be rid of this bothersome person. Yet still the sensation of "someone's missing" is present, and it is further exacerbated by an even heavier one—a sensation of guilt because that person has not been given a worthy place.

These sensations are evident to some people, although they may go unnoticed by the majority. Regardless of whether you acknowledge them or not, these sensations begin to tug on you and direct your life unconsciously. It is as if you are a puppet being pulled about by invisible threads.

Who Belongs to the Family?

When I speak of including all your family members, you might think I'm referring to the people you have a blood bond with. You might even be including the children that your spouse had with his former spouse, who are your adopted offspring. It's very probable that your list includes that soul mate you call "sister" and the uncle who, though not a brother to either of your parents, is very important to you because he's been present at all your birthday celebrations. A large component of my students include the pets in their family, and I understand them perfectly because I adored my dog. His death hurt more than the passing of my maternal grandfather, whom I barely knew.

Believe me when I say I know that what I'm going to explain now might be very difficult to accept at the beginning, but it can also be profoundly revealing and healing. When I say "all members of the family," I am considering only those who take part in the invisible family legacy. Specifically, that includes the following:

- all children (including aborted, dead, stillborn, half siblings, and children given up for adoption)
- parents and all their siblings
- grandparents and their siblings
- great grandparents and their siblings.
- ancestors and their siblings
- persons who, although not relatives, had misfortunes that benefited some family members
- persons who left a space clear for someone in the family to occupy (for example, the former spouses of parents or grandparents)

- perpetrators of offenses against someone in the family
- victims of someone in the family

You may be surprised by the inclusion of those last four groups, and the omission of others who seem to have a more rightful place on the list. Without knowing it, you've been including those who do not belong and excluding members of your family system, and when this occurs, the flow of life energy is cut short and tragic stories get repeated.

Every member of the family has a place, and if he or she is not allowed to occupy it, another family member will fill in that gap and repeat that story of pain. That's why it's important for you to recognize who belongs to your family and allow that individual to take his or her place. If you do not, you or someone you love will suffer through the same story as the excluded one.

Understanding your family members is essential, so I'll explain in detail who belongs to your family for the purposes of this book and therefore needs to be included.

All Children

Normally, only children who are alive and who are present in the family are counted; others are not mentioned. But all children anchor you to life, and when they are excluded, they do exactly the opposite of that—they anchor you to death. Anchoring you to life is equal to making decisions and taking actions that are good for you, nourish you, and give you joy. Anchoring you to death means that you will feel an attraction to that which is harmful to you. This is a very broad topic that I will deal with later on; for the moment, focus on understanding who belongs to your family system, and then you will see how excluding children affects you.

Abortions

This refers to children who were not wanted and so the pregnancy was interrupted. Taking the facts as they are, an abortion is equivalent to taking the life of someone who is just starting out. Abortions affect the family system in several ways, one of which is that these children are normally not counted and so cause a disturbance in the order between siblings.

For example, if there was an abortion and then two children, only the two live children are generally counted, but in fact the first one was the aborted one, followed by the others. So the second child occupies the place of the firstborn who carries an energy of death and murder, because his or her death was provoked. This sounds very dramatic, but it needs to be acknowledged in all its truth, given the implications it carries.

The good thing is that this has a solution once you recognize the problem. If you're feeling uncomfortable because you don't know if there was an abortion before you came along, or you had an abortion and don't want this to affect your children, relax. The first step is acknowledging the problem.

Abortions also affect the couple's relationship, creating a separation or a breakup. After an abortion, it is common to see one partner keeping his or her distance or breaking off the relationship. After some time, they either come back together or terminate the relationship definitively. The burden of death that an abortion generates depends on the circumstances in which it took place and the pain it provoked. Spontaneous abortions are treated as dead children.

Dead Children

When a child dies, it causes a great deal of pain for the family. It's the natural order of things for parents to die before their children. When children lose their parents when they are little, they are called orphans. However, there is no word defining the parents who lose a child.

Given the pain of losing a child to death, every member of the family responds differently. Some hang on to their pain or allow themselves to be swallowed up by it and neglect their live children or their spouse. Others deny the pain and act as if nothing happened.

When a child dies in the womb, during childbirth, or during the first year of life, the next child to be born is often given the name of the firstborn, as if this child were meant to replace the child who died.

Repeating names is a problem when it's done to hang on to that family member who is no longer around. The member who carries this name feels obligated to carry on with what was expected of that other person throughout life. This is done unconsciously out of love for the family.

One action can have many meanings, so if you've given your two children the same name, or if you carry someone else's name, there are ways of assigning a positive meaning to this. You'll find many ways in this book to reformulate a family tragedy to a happy outcome. A heavy load can become a blessing with the right resources. For example, imagine that among those who carry the same name there is such a special bond that the dead one is blessing the other from that special place he or she abides in. Say to yourself that it is an honor to carry the same name and that you're freed from suffering through what that individual suffered through. There is no need for further pain.

This makes the fact that names are repeated in your family no longer negative. I do still think it best, though, for every child to have a different name, symbolizing the unique and special place he or she holds in the family.

Half Siblings

Half siblings share a mother or a father, but not both. These are the children born out of a previous relationship or a relationship that was going on at the same time. Children contain both their biological parents. In order to keep them in a good place, both parents need to be included. That's the issue when half siblings are concerned, as the other mother or father will generally be excluded. I explain this in greater detail in the section on taking life energy from the ancestors.

The story of the "other partner" is laden with emotions when dealing with this particular child. It's quite common for that child to be given an inadequate place as compensation, sometimes higher than the offspring these parents have in common, sometimes lower. Both choices are harmful, for this is not a worthy place where the child is respected for who he or she is, nor for the other parent. If the father or mother of this child generates shame or guilt, the child carries it. If there is anger against the father or the mother, the child will be treated aggressively.

If the father or the mother is absent because of some sad story, the child will be pitied.

As a result, this child is not treated as an equal to the other children, yet all children are equal in value and deserve to be respected within their true lineage without denying their origin. A half sibling is included when his or her biological parent is included—that is, when the father or the mother is also acknowledged to be part of the family. The big problem in trying to do this is the stories and tangled-up sentiments relative to the father or the mother of the half sibling. One parent looking at that child sees the other parent, and all those sentiments get triggered.

For this reason, many parents in this situation prefer to forget the existence of the other parent and deny him or her. By doing this, they cause harm to the child and exclude the child because if they don't respect the biological parent, they therefore don't respect this child. This child's biological parents live within this child, both of them, even if one of the parents is absent or you don't believe that parent deserves respect. Including the parent of this child is a show of love for him or her.

Children Given Up for Adoption

Adoption is often kept a secret, and neither the spouse nor the other children know about it. How can you include someone you don't know exists? If your spouse, either of your parents, or an ancestor gave a child up for adoption, you'll be relying on those family members to be the ones to tell you. Additionally, you'll be unwittingly excluding that child. If you gave a child up for adoption, you probably think about it often and ask yourself what that child's life is like. You may feel guilt, remorse, apprehension, nostalgia, or something similar. All this weighs the invisible family legacy down further.

And what about adopted children? They belong to their own biological family. The problem is that the adoptive parents give them the place of biological offspring and, unknowingly, exclude their own children and the biological family of their adopted children. For example, a couple wants to have children, tries repeatedly, and has two natural abortions (miscarriages). They finally adopt a child and then manage to give birth to a child. They now have three biological offspring: the two natural abortions and the one who managed to live. The adopted child does not belong to this family system but is affected by occupying the place of the firstborn, when this place belongs to the first aborted child.

It's not about treating these children differently or about the amount of love you have for your children. In practice, a generous heart gifts love and care equally to all adopted offspring, to a spouse's children, and to all biological offspring. However, it's important to give the corresponding place to each member of the family system in order for there to be peace and harmony. The best thing for a child is to be included in his or her biological family. To do this, you might simply imagine the biological parents standing behind the child and honor this image in your mind. The biological bonds remain, and all the offspring in your family system abide in your heart, whether you know them or not.

Parents and All Their Siblings

Life comes to you from your parents, and they take it from their parents and from their siblings. The way this works is as follows: your parents take life from their ancestors and from their eldest siblings; they give each other life energy; and they pass that energy on to their first offspring. The second child takes life from the parents and from the older sibling. The third child takes life from the parents and from the two older siblings, and so on. The energy of life flows from top to bottom, from ancestors to progeny, and from older siblings to younger siblings. When your father, mother, or some uncle or aunt does not occupy the rightful place, the flow of life energy is cut off and does not reach you.

We call someone an excluded member when he or she does not occupy the proper place in the family system. This can happen for a number of reasons. Here are just a few relative to your parents:

- Your father or your mother is not present because he or she died or abandoned you.

- Your parents gave you up for adoption, and you've considered your adoptive family to be the one and only real family for you.

- You have no information about your biological father or mother.

- Your mother does not approve of your father, and you don't include him out of love for her.

- Your father does not approve of your mother, and you don't include her out of love for him.

- One of your parents scorns the family of origin of the other, and so you exclude this branch from your lineage.

- Your paternal grandparents reject your mother, so you don't have permission to give her, her place.

- Your maternal grandparents reject your father, so you must choose between giving your maternal grandparents their place or your father.

The entanglements between parents and grandparents are dealt with in-depth in the section on how to take life energy from your ancestors. For now, I simply want you to get an idea of how easy it is to exclude your parents and their siblings and the negative effect this has for you.

Your aunts and uncles are excluded when you don't count them as equals in your parents' line of siblings. Reasons for this to occur include the following:

- They don't get along with your parents.

- They died when they were little.

- They got married, and their spouse rejected the family of origin.

- They are half siblings to one of your parents.

- They were aborted or given up for adoption, and you aren't even aware of their existence.

- They have some trait that generates conflict for the family— for example, homosexuality, a disease that the family finds shameful (madness, drug addiction), or living in a way that runs counter to the family's established values.

Your parents and aunts or uncles may be excluded even when your relationship with them is good. Including someone does not imply the need to get along with them behaviorally. As we go further along, you'll understand what all this means. For now, you're discovering how gaps can exist within your family system, and in recognizing these you are starting your process of healing.

Grandparents and Their Siblings

You take life from your mother, your father, and your siblings. Your mother and your father take life from their parents and from their siblings. Your grandparents take it from their parents and from their siblings. If any of these are excluded in the family system, they do not take the full measure of life energy and, therefore, neither do you.

For every family member who is missing, less life energy comes to you, and other entanglements occur of which I will speak later. As you've already identified the problem, you're on the right path in your process of transformation.

Great Grandparents and Their Siblings

So far, I believe the panorama is very clear. Imagine a great waterfall that instead of water carries life energy, luminous and brilliant, with sparkles of light that twinkle like stars. All that life energy comes to you complete when every member of the family is included.

Imagine that from your eight great-grandparents and from all their siblings, life energy descends toward your four grandparents and all great-uncles and aunts, and from each one of them it passes on to your parents, aunts, and uncles. All receive the full force of life energy and pass it on complete. It accumulates and multiplies with every member of the family.

Now your parents pass it on to you, and you receive it completely. You also multiply it and pass it on to and receive it from your siblings, in accordance with your place in the family. This flow of life energy is happening harmoniously and easily, merely in discovering what it means to include your parents, aunts, uncles, grandparents, great aunts, great uncles, great grandparents, and their siblings. All are integrated and included, and all take their proper place, even though you never met them and they are new to the family. Every member is welcomed by all the others and feels honored to belong to your family. You look at this image with a smile on your face.

Ancestors and Their Siblings

Your family system stretches back generation upon generation to your remotest forefathers. All of them have taken life from parents, siblings, and spouse to pass on to their progeny. As such, life continues to be passed on from generation to generation, and in every person live all their ancestors. Take a look at the following chart to get an idea of the number of ancestors who live in you:

You	1
Parents	2
Grandparents	4
Great grandparents	8
Great great grandparents	16
Great great great grandparents	32
6th ascending generation	64
7th ascending generation	128
8th ascending generation	256
9th ascending generation	512
10th ascending generation	1,024
11th ascending generation	2,048
12th ascending generation	4,096
13th ascending generation	8,192
14th ascending generation	16,384
15th ascending generation	32,768
16th ascending generation	65,536
17th ascending generation	131,072
18th ascending generation	262,144

19th ascending generation	524,288
20th ascending generation	1,048,576
Total ancestors	2,097,150

Only parents were calculated in this chart, not siblings, because that is a different story for every family.

When your ancestors are included, life energy is abundant. The more life energy there is, the better for you and for your progeny. How do you include your ancestors? Remember, the first step is recognizing the problem. At this point, you are fully aware of how you have forgotten them or perhaps some of them. Sometimes there are branches of the family tree that have been lost.

Pay special attention to those who suffered through a tragic story. Expect to find that the logic of family systems is quite illogical for some people. For example, it is considered a tragic story to have had too many children or none at all. Having too many children may be considered tragic because when this occurs, many of the children die, and the mother is weakened or gets sick. Not having children is considered tragic because no life courses through that family. Of course, people can compensate for this through a profession that gives life meaning, so life energy is shared through one's work instead.

Other examples of tragic stories include:

- losing parents during infancy

- children abandoned because of a death, illness, war, or for any other reason

- rape or abuse

- living in poverty

- illnesses

- abandonment and loneliness

- physical and emotional pain

- suicide

- tragic death (untimely death)

- accidents

- some physical or mental limitation

When an ancestor suffers and the members of the family do not see or acknowledge the pain experienced, the story will be repeated time and again. The solution is in acknowledging what occurred without adding to it or detracting from it. The more the ancestor suffered, the more respect he or she must be given. The amount of respect must be equivalent to the amount of pain suffered. Recognizing the stories of tragedy and giving all members of the family their place is where your healing lies.

How can you know who to respect if you barely know anything about your ancestors' stories? How are pain and respect measured? How are you going to be able to heal your family? If you're torturing yourself with these questions, take a deep breath and let it out, releasing all that anxiety. Remember that in the Magui Block Method, there are three movements for achieving a positive change: you identify the entanglement—that is, that which has got you stuck; you identify the solution; and you transform it as if by magic. This is the section on including your family. You're still on the first step, identifying what has kept you stuck. How many years have you had this problem? There were excluded ancestors already before you were born, so there's no hurry. You'll reach the magic, I can assure you!

The information you will receive below may surprise you, but if you open your mind and heart, you'll be able to integrate it with ease and joy.

Persons Whose Misfortune Benefited the Family

This refers to all those persons, even those not related to you, whose misfortune was an advantage to someone in the family. Let me share some real-life stories.

A woman gets sick and requires medical attention. Her family has already spent all the money they had and are willing to get more by selling their business, house, and two cars. They've worked hard for years to accumulate these things, but they're willing to give it all up for the sake of their loved one's health. They sell everything in a hurry. Their relative is seriously ill and needs treatment.

The people who purchase all this get it for an extraordinary price. Imagine: a fully functioning business at an incredible price, a beautiful house created and inhabited by love for a song, and two cars that are in good shape at a price you'd not get anywhere else. They made an offer, and it was accepted. It was an opportunity, and they took advantage of it; this is how business works. They might not even have known why the owners were in such a rush to sell everything, for it was not their problem, was it? Other people's misfortunes have nothing to do with us, or so we believe, and we all like to get a bargain. This is the perfect formula for adding weight to your family legacy.

In the European countries occupied by the Nazis during the Second World War, many Jewish families lost their properties, goods, and money. Those losses for the Jews were gains for other families. There are people who enjoy these goods now without having any idea of who their original owners were and how the items were acquired.

I remember a German family in which all members but one died tragically in terrible accidents or by acquiring deadly diseases. The only living member left was fifty-five years old and completely alone. Oh, yes, she was a millionaire. She did some investigating and realized she was a millionaire thanks to a business her grandfather "bought" from a Jew who was put into a concentration camp together with all his family. This Jewish family's misfortune was to her family's advantage, but it was paid for dearly and for generations afterward.

This is the way family systems work. The tragic stories of excluded members are visited upon other family members. Two families who apparently have no relation to one another are connected when a member of one family takes advantage of the misfortune of the other. If the intention is to cause harm, this weighs even heavier, but a link exists either way. The German family ended up disappearing, just as the Jewish family did.

What can you do? The obvious thing is to stop taking advantage of someone else's suffering, yet we do this without even realizing it. Let me give you a personal example.

I live in Mexico, and my financial status allows me to hire a house cleaner to help out with the chores at home. In terms of salary, one hour of my work is equivalent to twenty-five hours of hers. This is how huge the discrepancy is in income, and it is common here. For many years, I mused over this and felt that I was taking advantage of this employee's misfortune. What was the result? Every house cleaner I hired stole money from me. My thoughts about things being uneven led them to take from me what they considered theirs. Why? Because I was not honoring them.

When you honor people, you treat them with dignity, and you acknowledge what they are supposed to experience in this lifetime. You also respect what you are meant to experience. You cannot balance out all the wrongs on this planet Earth. From the moment I got this, I have enjoyed having an excellent and honest house cleaner who makes more money than others in the market. We both feel in balance, and nobody is taking advantage of the other. You get the difference?

Allowing people to carry their load in life, although it might be a difficult one, means you give them their place and you honor it. Taking advantage of someone's misfortune and obtaining a benefit from it is a different thing. So look at the people you are surrounded by and feel profound respect for them without trying to compensate for how difficult their life might be or has been.

Persons Who Left a Place Free for Someone Else

This refers to those who left a place free so that someone else in the family could occupy it—for example, the former spouses of your parents, grandparents, or other ancestors. How do we include these others? It's very easy! Look at how I do this.

My father and his girlfriend broke up so that he could go to school in Paris. There he met my mother. My father's first girlfriend left the place free for my mother to occupy. I thank and honor my father's first girlfriend because she opened up the space in my father's life for me to be born. My father's first girlfriend belongs to my family, and I recognize her place within it. I also imagine that my mother recognizes her as my father's first girlfriend. It's simpler than you thought, isn't it?

The only thing you do with these people is take them into account and recognize that thanks to the fact that they are no longer there, your family is just as it is. They played a part in your family's story, they belong in the system, and until they are included, the number is incomplete.

Your former partners and your partner's former partners also form part of your family. Thanks to the fact that those relationships did not work out, you and your partner are free to be together. If you have no partner at present, you still must include your former partners, for in this manner you open up to a new story without carrying someone else's load. So bless them, be thankful they are no longer there, and give them a good place. All former partners belong to the family system. Thanks to the fact that they've gone, new partnerships were formed that brought life and well-being.

Who is considered a partner? One thing that defines a couple relationship is the sexual connection, regardless of whether or not you consider this important. If you had so many that it's difficult to keep count, you take the ones most significant to you using the logic of family systems. Let me explain: what weighs the heaviest are issues of life and death. That's why it's important to count the relationships that included pregnancies, whether or not they went to full term, and whether or not there were abortions or deaths. If you had a violent relationship, no matter its duration, it's important you include it. The relationships in which you and the other person ended up feeling resentful also need to be counted in.

There is a tendency to count only the couple relationships that you consider important, but the heavier ones for the family are most likely the ones you're *not* counting: the excluded ones. If you're in doubt, you'd better include them as a partner and include them in the family. That's much better than having to repeat a story that does not work. Just by acknowledging them as part of your story, their stories no longer have to be repeated. You don't forget what you learn well.

If your history is one with many couple relationships, it may be hard to keep count. What to do when the tally does not match? What to do when you don't know the partners of other members of the family? It's enough for you to recognize that all those who make space for another to arrive are part of the family. This attitude is inclusive and complies with the laws of the family system. Sometimes they just cannot be counted. The most important thing is not the number, it's the attitude of respect that creates space for them to belong and allows for peace to reign.

Imagine that you're eating out in a restaurant and don't greet a member of your family because you're looking out the window. Your relative gets that you are not greeting her because you don't see her. Now imagine you're looking straight at this person but your attitude is one that says of them, "You do not belong to the family." Your relative will then feel resentful. The same thing applies to the attitude of inclusion or exclusion. If you look at someone, such your grandfather's lover, but treat her as if she were not part of the family, she feels resentful, and the family legacy is further weighed down.

What is healing for you is the internal attitude of, "I honor all those who belong to my family, for even though I don't know them, they have a good place in my heart." Your heart will grow ever more exponentially capable when you include all the members of your family.

Perpetrators of an Offense Against Someone in the Family

A perpetrator is someone who commits an offense against family members, whether it be against their goods or their person. Those individuals now belong to the family system. The greater the damage done by the perpetrator, the more it affects the family when he or she is excluded. Remember that what we're preventing is a constant repeat of those tragic stories.

When you include someone in the family who did you harm, the message is, "I give you a place because what you did was very serious, and nobody should carry that but you." Then you imagine the perpetrators carrying their own heavy burden of responsibility for what they did—all 100 percent of their actions. If you don't give perpetrators a place because you feel someone who is that bad does not deserve to belong to the family, who's going to carry the weight of the damage done? Some other person will take responsibility, and as this does not work, the story will be repeated. Only when the one who committed the offense recognizes the gravity of his or her actions will the burden be carried correctly.

You hold a lot of power in your mind, so use it in your favor. Imagine that all perpetrators are included, you and everyone accepts that they form part of the family, and you give them an important place—the greater the damage done, the more important the place. The perpetrators take it, and this means that they assume full responsibility. They look at the victim and at all the people they have harmed through their actions, and they are remorseful for what they did. They realize how much damage they have done and are sorry. In this way, you include the perpetrators, and they take their place in the family, carry the weight of their actions, and profoundly lament what they did.

This is the well-ordered picture, and you're now integrating it. This well-ordered picture is multiplied until it includes all the perpetrators in your family system. Every perpetrator is included in the family, assumes personal responsibility, looks at the victim, and declares regret.

Later on, you'll gain a better understanding of perpetrators and victims. For now, you're including all those who have harmed someone in the family, and you are liberating yourself from what corresponds to them. You deserve this, and you do this for yourself and for your family.

Victims of Someone in the Family

These are the people who were harmed by someone in the family, regardless of the intention. For example, there's an accident at the family's factory, and several employees are hurt or killed. These victims and their families now belong to the family system, and they need to be honored.

Perhaps a grandfather participated in a war and has a medal. He is considered a hero in town, but he may very well have killed several of the enemy, don't you think? These enemies who were killed belong to the family system. If one of the uncles ends up being a pedophile, the children he abused are also part of the family.

When you include the victims, you stop repeating stories and can walk through life feeling safe. Imagine all the victims in your family being included and treated with great respect. Their perpetrators look at them and say, "I'm sorry." They look at their perpetrators and receive an apology. Something calms down in their heart. Now there is peace in the family. The victims have been included.

The work required to heal victims and perpetrators is very profound, and you'll gain a greater awareness of it in the section on cycles of violence. In the meantime, you can be satisfied to know the victims have a good place and that their story has been concluded. Why? Because you've created that picture in your mind. There are more steps about this, which you will follow later.

How to Include Someone into Your Family

You now have the list of all those who must be included in the family. When you leave someone out, that person is being excluded from your family system. All those members of the family who are denied membership into the system—their honor and equality of rank—are considered excluded. There are three factors here:

- *Membership in the system*—Recognize that these individuals are part of the family. Sometimes you don't know them because you did not know they were part of the family or because you don't know them. Whether you do it deliberately or not, you exclude them, and there are repercussions from that.

- *Honoring*—This refers to treating someone with respect. All members must be honored—that is, respected with regard to what is meant to be theirs to experience. The more tragic that person's life story is, the more respect he or she must be given. You exclude members of your family when you do not treat them with due respect in accordance with their life experience, whether by playing down their pain or by feeling sorry for them.

- *Equality of rank*—All family members must have the hierarchy that corresponds to the place they occupy in the family. You exclude them when you do not respect them in the place they occupy within the family system. For example, a partner has to have the same hierarchy as the other partners. A brother has to receive the same respect as the other siblings.

It's common for there to be excluded members in a family without the others noticing. For example, a brother is born with a disability, and for some of the siblings it's as if he does not exist. For others, he does belong, but he does not have the same rank as the other siblings. Some might feel sorry for him, and they don't know what to do with this brother.

When there is a healing movement and the internal picture regarding that brother is changed, the other siblings will have clarity with regard to the right actions to take. The brother with the disability will be included in the line of siblings as an equal in rank and honored much more than the others because his life story is heavy. When the siblings do this, there is peace in the family.

These factors apply to every member of the family. Your "including" needs to be done in the following way for all: knowing they belong, honoring them according to their story, and giving them the rank they have.

How do you do this? Well, you already have the list of all those who belong to your family, and you have created healing images in your mind for including them with honor and giving them the correct rank. At the end of the chapter, you will be grounding all this by uniting your mind, your body, and your emotions. Throughout the book, you'll be learning more tools. And now, I'm going to give you a great motivator.

What Happens When You Don't Include Them All?

When a member of a family system is excluded, another member feels a tug and needs to make a place for that individual in the system. It's like the example of the tour group. The group has been traveling together for months, and some members have established bonds between them. Suddenly, one member does not arrive in time to board the bus. The ones who feel a special bond with that member of the group will feel pulled upon and will not rest easy until the missing one occupies his or her place. If someone in your family is missing because they've been excluded, some members will feel a pull and identify with the missing one.

A family identification means that a member unconsciously carries the excluded member and repeats that person's story. The objective of this is for the excluded member to be included. What one is seeking unconsciously is for that member to be acknowledged as belonging and to have his or her experiences honored and rank respected. The problem is that all this takes place unconsciously, out of blind love. The bond with that member of the family is invisible; it is not seen but felt.

When a person identifies with an excluded member, he or she does so by using one of the following dynamics:

- *I follow you*—In this dynamic, the excluded one's story is repeated. For example, in the case of an aunt who never married, the niece who identifies with her will not get married either.

- *I do it instead of you*—In this dynamic, the person who has the identification wants to save the excluded one and does what the other was unable to do. For example, the child perceives that his father is going to get sick, and he gets sick first. Here the son is living under the illusion that by getting sick, he's preventing his father from getting sick and gives him a place in the family. In another example, the grandmother got married and had a bunch of children, but she really wanted to study and travel the world; the granddaughter has a doctorate, is successful professionally, and travels a lot, but she does not get married or have children. She is unconsciously complying with what her grandmother wished. The problem is not that she does not get married or have children; what is damaging is that she does this because of her identification with her grandmother, so she is not free to choose even though it might seem that she is.

- *Expiation*—The one who identifies with the excluded member sacrifices himself or herself by suffering through the same thing as the excluded member, though externally there is no reason to do so. An example of this would be that of a great-grandfather who suffered from poverty and hunger. Even though the

43

grandson has money and food in abundance, he does not enjoy them but feels anxious when he eats, is a workaholic, and is worried about his finances, living as if he were poor. In this way, he's giving his ancestor a place.

Identifications generally take place in the first few years of life, before the age of seven, which is why they can mark people so. Imagine growing up carrying around a load that corresponds to someone else. How free can you be to choose what you want to experience?

This is why there are very positive changes that take place when you include all those who belong to your family and honor their story and rank. With this new awareness, you're going to achieve a profound transformation.

Apply the Magui Block Method to Include Them All

You've taken the first step by identifying the entanglement. With everything you've learned, you know your family has members who have been excluded. The second step is identifying the solution: including them. During your reading, you created images that began transforming what was happening in your family, and now you're going to ground the work done to achieve the magic.

First, adopt the right physical posture, as follows:

- Hold your body upright. Imagine that your head is touching the sky and that your feet are firmly and deeply grounded in the earth.

- Be centered. Your heart and mind are as clear as crystal.

- Place your hands, one over the other, on your belly button. Imagine that they connect to the space that is close to your spine, inside of your body. (If you're a woman, place the palm of your right hand on your belly button and the palm of the left hand on the back of your right hand. If you're a man, place the palm of your left hand on your belly button and the palm of the right hand on the back of your left hand.)

Next, evoke love:

- Remember your willingness to heal, and smile.

- Feel appreciation for yourself.

- Be thankful for the moment.

Finally, appreciate the power of these words :

- Repeat these phrases out loud.

- Listen to the way you say them, and repeat them until they come naturally to you.

Now, adopt the right posture, evoke love, and repeat the following out loud:

> *I include all those who belong in my family.*
> *All are included.*
> *All belong.*
> *The number is complete.*
> *Even though I don't know them, I include them now.*
> *I include all the offspring: the products of abortions, the ones who died, the stillborn, the half siblings, and those given up for adoption.*
> *I include my parents and all their siblings.*
> *I include my maternal grandparents and their siblings.*
> *I include my paternal grandparents and their siblings.*
> *I include my maternal great grandparents and their siblings.*
> *I include my paternal great grandparents and their siblings.*
> *I include my ancestors and their siblings.*
> *I include all those whose misfortune benefited the family.*
> *I honor them, though I am not aware of what happened, and I am sorry for their misfortune.*
> *I include all those who left a space free for someone else.*

I include all the partners I've had and stop repeating painful stories.
I include the partners my partner has had.
I include my family members' partners.
I include the perpetrators—all those who have brought harm to someone in the family.
I include the victims—all those who have been harmed by someone in the family.
I now include all the members of my family, and peace reigns.
The number is complete.
All belong and are honored.
I honor their life stories.
I give them their place in the family and honor their rank.
And the painful stories have ended.
I include all the members of my family, and peace reigns.
The number is complete.
All belong and are honored.
I honor their life stories.
The painful stories are over.
All are included in my family, and peace reigns.
The number is complete.
All belong and are honored.
I honor their life stories.
And the pain is over.
So be it, so it is.

Key #2: Get Your Family in Order

A family is in order when all of its members occupy their corresponding place and perform their own function. Imagine an orchestra: before performing for the public, all the musicians take their seats, take up their instruments, look at their score, and prepare to play the correct part when the moment is right. Each musician has the specific score for the instrument he or she plays. The members are seated in the group in such a way that the sound can be heard beautifully. Everything has an order and a reason for being, though only those in the know are aware of this. In order for there to be harmony, every musician has to accept his or her specific place within the system and play the corresponding score.

The same thing happens in a well-ordered family. All members occupy their own place and take charge of their corresponding function. This can become complex because the place and the function change depending on the connection.

For example, Jessica occupies the following places in her family: daughter to her parents, wife to her husband, mother to her children, younger sister to her older brother, and older sister to her younger brother. In each of these roles, she has a different function. In order for her family to remain in order, she is only allowed to be what she is in each relationship. But in practice, Jessica finds it much more difficult to be what she is than to do what is asked of her.

When her father has one of those events to go to that her mother hates, Jessica accompanies him; instead of being her father's daughter, she plays the role of his partner at the party. This happens often, so she takes on this role. However, Jessica needs to be her parents' daughter because that is her place.

Since this gap has existed from infancy, she places herself in the role of the daughter with her husband, in the hope of receiving from him what she did not receive from her own parents. Consequently, she throws spectacular tantrums when he doesn't buy her what she wants. When she does this, she puts herself in the place of a sister to their children and relinquishes her authority to raise them. Nor can she get along well with her siblings because she puts herself above them, as if she were their mother.

The minute you leave your place, you stop exercising your function, and everything gets complicated. The worst part is that you also complicate things for everyone else. No member can occupy a rightful place with serenity while someone is trying to take it away or specify how he or she should be doing things differently.

To get your family in order, you need to understand the elements that make it up, how and why families get out of order, what happens when this occurs, and then how to resolve it. You're going to learn this quickly and easily by applying the Magui Block Method. Remember that a family is in order when each member occupies his or her place and does what he or she is supposed to do.

The Elements of Order

There are three elements we will take into account in ordering the family: time, function, and the soul weight of each of the members in the system. These three elements are combined to create the perfect order.

Time

There are two criteria to the element of time.

First in Time, First in Rights.

The first one to enter the system is the one with the most rights and obligations. This is easy to understand through the following examples:

- *A couple is formed and then come the children.* In a well-ordered family, the couple has time to nourish itself, and intimate spaces are acknowledged. In a family that is out of order, the children take precedence over the parents and take up so much space that the couple's relationship is drained. This is equivalent to putting the children between the two parents, apparently protected and sustained by their parents, such as when a couple walks through a park taking their child by the hand between them. It looks sweet and is a pleasant way to get along, but only for walking through the park. In life, the couple must walk hand in hand, with nobody between them, not even their children.

  Manuel is Patricia and Marco's eldest son. They like to sleep with him, and it seems much more comfortable for them to have him in their bed to keep him calm when he wakes up at night. This they've done since he was born, and it has worked for them. Manuel is now seven—the same as the number of years that this couple has gone without sex. This is one of the prices this couple's relationship pays in allowing the family system to be out of order. But the price the son pays is worse. Manuel has many fears, and this is why they have to come to me for therapy.

When parents put their children above their couple relationship, the children carry the parents and suffer. You'll learn more about this later on. For now, understand the criteria regarding the first in the family system having more rights and obligations than those who come later. There is a reason for this which you will discover very soon.

- *The first child has more rights and obligations than the second.* In a well-ordered family, the siblings respect the hierarchy that corresponds to each of them in accordance with their order of arrival, where the best is sought for all. The eldest brother looks out for the interests of his younger siblings and respects every one of them. In a family that is out of order, some of the siblings set themselves above the others, try to order the others about, stomp all over them, or assume rights that do not correspond to their place in the family.

Present Relationships Have Priority over Previous Ones

You are living in the here and now, and leaving the past behind. This is easy to understand with the following examples:

- *The second and current couple take precedence over the first couple.* Juan has three children by Sandra, gets divorced, and then marries Veronica. The couple relationship with Sandra no longer exists. His current partner is Veronica, and she is the only one who should occupy that place.

  Here we're going to combine the two criteria: *first in time, first in rights* and *present relationships have priority*. Veronica is Juan's partner, yet before she came into Juan's life, there were three children. Sandra is the mother of those children and is still occupying that place in Juan's life. If Sandra recognizes that her place is as the children's mother and not as his partner, she can have a good relationship with him and with Veronica. If Veronica respects that she is only Juan's partner and not the mother of their children, Sandra will feel honored and secure in her place.

Juan needs to recognize the place each holds, otherwise he will feel pulled in all directions by each of the members of the system. If Juan thinks that when Sandra seeks him out it's because she still wants him as her partner, he'll be on the defensive and unable to team up with her for the sake of the children. Order is simple when all know their own place and that of each of the others.

- *The current family takes precedence over your family of origin.* Your family of origin is made up of your parents, your siblings, and your ancestors. The current family refers to your partner and your children. You receive life from your family of origin and pass it on to your current family. Your parents are important, but your greatest commitment is to your children.

  Mariana would like to get married and have a family of her own, but her mother is widowed and very lonely. Every time Mariana starts up a couple relationship, her mother gets sick. What should Mariana do? In order to know, you need to learn the second element for putting your family in order.

Function

This second element of order refers to the role the member plays within the system (for example, current partner, child, mother, father, older sibling, previous partner). There is order when the members of a family play the roles that correspond to their place in the family. If we return to the example of the orchestra, each musician must play his or her own instrument.

Consider the previous example: why does Mariana's mother get sick every time her daughter has a boyfriend? Because she is occupying the role of her daughter's partner, and the idea of losing her partner again is too painful. What can Mariana do? What she must do is occupy the role of daughter and accept that the role of partner for her mother is empty. If the mother feels lonely, she can open up to having a new relationship, but this gap will never be filled as long as Mariana continues to occupy it.

Mariana is only the daughter; no matter how hard she tries, she will not be able to take up a different role than her own, as much as she wants to make her mother happy. She is more helpful to her mother if she leads the life she desires. If she removes herself from the role of partner, the mother will have to face her emptiness and decide whether to live alone or together with a new partner. Order is easy when all family members know what their function is and exercise it.

How can we manage the pain caused by empty places in the family? This leads us to the third element in getting the family in order.

Soul Weight

Soul weight refers to a person's maturity of soul. Soul weight is obtained through experiences in life—by facing the pain of loss and difficult stories. You gain in soul weight when you assume what is yours to live, face it with dignity and without victimizing yourself, and do something good with your life. Soul weight is also obtained by taking from and honoring your parents, as you will see in the section on taking life energy from your ancestors.

The objective of these three elements—time, function, and soul weight—is for each member to occupy his or her place within the system and be honored. This hierarchy is observed in internal attitudes and in the way family members are treated. It never refers to the value of the person or to the time and devotion he or she are given. For example, though a son may be last in hierarchy, if he is a little child, he will receive more attention and care than his older sibling.

How and Why Are Families Knocked Out of Order?

A family can get out of order in the following ways:

- *A member leaves his or her place and stops exercising his or her function.* In the example of the orchestra, this is equivalent to musicians leaving their spot and their instrument lying about.

- *One member takes the place of another, trying to take on a function that does not belong to him or her.* In the example of the orchestra, this is equivalent to a musician taking the place of another musician and taking that colleague's instrument from him or her. The musician in question might try to play his or her own instrument and that of the other musician, hopping from one place to the other, trying to comply with what needs to be played in both musical scores. It might also be that the musician will put down his or her own instrument to play the other's.

In both cases, the entire family system is affected.

When a place remains empty, all family members feel the gap and the tug to fill it. If they do that, their own place will be left empty. This creates even more disorder because several members will try to fill that gap. The problem is that the only person who can occupy it is the original owner. Even though others might leave their own place and try to fill that void, nobody has the capacity to do so.

Each member of the family is like a piece of a jigsaw puzzle, cut to certain specifications. Only one piece fits in that gap. You can try to get others to fit, but the only one that is going to fit right in is the one that has the exact shape. This is what happens with the members of a family. Only the original member can occupy his or her own space and exercise the corresponding function.

Let's analyze each case because the first step in healing is identifying the entanglement; after that, it's much easier to transform it.

Members Leave Their Place and Stop Exercising Their Function

This happens for many reasons. Family members die, leave, feel they can no longer cope with the burden, or perhaps do not like their place or function and refuse to take it on. Do you find this surprising?

Imagine an adolescent who gets pregnant when she's just starting to have some fun. Do you think she wants to be a mother and take care of a child? She may or may not; she might assume her responsibility as a mother and suddenly become a responsible adult, or she might have the child and continue having fun without taking on the role of mother.

What does taking your place or not taking it depend on? Free will, basically—but if your invisible family legacy is very heavy, you're not really free to choose. Without realizing it, you may be occupying someone else's place and taking on someone else's function. The roles you acquire in infancy do not always allow you to take the place that corresponds to who you are now. It's an illusion to believe you can occupy your spot and perform your own function if you're also taking someone else's place.

One Member Takes the Place of Another

There are situations in which you feel obliged to assume a responsibility or a role that does not correspond to your place in the family. At those times, you believe that it is right for you to do so, and you do it out of love for your family. You feel good when you do this. If you were to refuse, you'd feel awful and terribly guilty. The guilt is what makes you occupy the place of another family member. What you're not aware of are the consequences and how they affect the other members. Once you understand this, I can assure you, you will do things differently.

Arturo was fourteen years old when his father died. Though he was the youngest, he was the only son. There were two older sisters and his mother, whom he considered helpless, and so he took on the role of "man of the house." Everyone affirmed this role at the funeral. Was he free to choose? Now Arturo is thirty, and he is in a crisis. His girlfriend left him because he did not feel ready to be married. Why can't he get married? Because the place he continues to occupy in his family of origin is that of partner to his mother and father to his sisters. He can neither commit to another woman nor have children of his own.

When a father or a mother dies or leaves, what usually happens is that one of the offspring steps into that role. Sometimes it's evident that the son is playing the role of father or mother to his siblings because he is paying the household bills and/or tending to them. What generally is not seen is the way in which he becomes partner to his parent to prevent that parent from remaining single. This happens out of love, but it is blind love. Before healing can take place, it must be transformed into wise love. It is imperative that you understand how blind love works when a family is out of order.

When a father dies, the son feels the emptiness and his mother's and siblings' pain. He feels his mother is weak, as are his siblings. Someone has to support the family and perform the functions of the father: guiding and providing. When one member of the family feels stronger than the rest and believes he is more capable than the others of taking charge, he sacrifices himself out of blind love. He believes what he is doing is providing joy to his dead father (wherever he might be) and to his mother. Only when the son feels that the mother and siblings are strong will he drop the load and return to his own place.

In an orchestra, it does not work for musicians to leave their places, take their instruments, and read a different score. The piece would be played in a disorderly fashion, and it would sound terrible. Similarly, if a member of the family moves out of his or her place, that place is left empty, and someone else is going to feel compelled to leave his or her own place to fill in that gap. If a member of the family does not do what corresponds to his or her place, someone else must. This will create chaos in the system—the same chaos that would ensue in an orchestra if the musicians were to swap places.

If You Take the Place of Another Person, You Cannot Occupy Your Own

We have this crazy idea that we can do everything—that all it takes is real effort. There are tons of affirmations to confirm this, like "Love conquers all." This may be true, but when applied to family systems, are you talking about wise love or blind? Wise love accepts that each person has a specific place in the family with a specific corresponding function to perform; blind love wants to prevent family members from performing their own function in the name of "love."

Let me remind you that in reality, you're not helping the one you love; you're merely multiplying that individual's pain and not allowing him or her to learn. You are not learning either. You have your place and your role, and if you take on that of another, you won't be living your life from your own place, which is the only place you have.

When you are faced with a difficult situation, many questions pop up. What is your place? What are you supposed to take charge of? Where are the healthy limits? This can get to be very, very complicated. If there's a problem in the family with one member or several, how much can you participate? When is it wisest to step aside?

For example, consider a mother who is getting really old. She has several offspring, but only one of them looks out for her. The well-ordered thing would be for each of her offspring to take part in helping to care for her, which is their role and function. However, in practice, the functions are split between those who are available. If the only one to participate were to stop doing so, what would happen to the mother? This son feels stuck between a rock and a hard place. He might not have the audacity of his siblings; he might feel grateful to his mother; or maybe he is the only one who has the strength and the resources to help her out.

Sometimes, the ones who receive less from their parents are the ones who end up caring for the parents in old age. That's odd, don't you think? It's like they're doing their best now in the hope of getting what was not given them while they were little—but if they were not given it before, it's unlikely they'll receive it from their aging parent now. There is a lot of pain and sacrifice mixed in with their caring for the parent, and that includes bouts of anger and feelings of impotence or sadness. There is also some resentment toward the other siblings, especially those who were pampered and possibly still are.

When the son in the story above manages to shift internally, he can care for his mother out of love, without sacrificing himself. He will feel very good about himself. If he knows himself to be a good son, he'll feel he deserves blessings from heaven, and so they will rain down on him. You cannot force other family members to take their place or perform their function. If you try fighting them, convincing them, telling other members what they must do, you're not doing what you need to do, and you're adding to the disorder in the family.

Imagine one of the musicians in an orchestra trying to tell the other members of the orchestra how to play their instruments. This musician would leave his own place and stop playing his own instrument. Instead of helping, this would only create more disorder. Besides, each musician knows how to play his or her own instrument but is not so familiar with that of the others.

Of course, there are musicians who feel they are experts in all instruments, and there are even some who believe they would be much better at playing another's instrument. There are musicians who think they alone could play all the instruments in the orchestra. Those musicians create a lot of chaos in orchestras because instead of playing their own instrument and doing that well, they are focused on what the other musicians are doing and criticizing them, continually leaving their place to correct the other musicians' performance. Can you imagine the disaster that would ensue?

Are you like that musician, correcting the members of your family because they're not performing their function or worrying about the way they're doing things? Are you carrying what belongs to other members of the family? How can you let go of roles that do not belong to you? Every time you get a better grasp of the problem, it'll be easier for you to stop getting tangled up in the chaos.

What Happens When a Family Is Not in Order?

Love and Life Are Blocked

Imagine a house that is beautiful and perfectly built, with solid foundations and the maintenance up to date. Apparently all is well—however, the pipes are clogged. There is water in the cistern, but it's not reaching the bathrooms or the kitchen. Since the family that inhabits this house has many members, the lack of water makes the bathrooms smell bad and makes it impossible for the dishes to be washed, among other things. After a while, nobody wants to spend any time at home because, though they love each other, it's hard to live together and express what they're feeling when there's such a mess and the house can't be cleaned properly. In fact, they have everything they need to be fine. They only need to unclog the pipes, and presto!

You replicate what you learned in your family of origin. If during the first years of your life you occupied a place that was different from the one that corresponds to you, you'll keep doing that in all your relationships. This is what you are familiar with; it is your comfort zone. For example, when Alicia was little, she learned to be mother to her mother. Why? Because her maternal grandmother was very busy and not present for the raising of her children. Since her infancy, Alicia felt her mother's need, and out of blind love occupied this place.

Alicia took on the role of adult when she was just a child. This role became her comfort zone, and it's hard for her to be the little child. Without realizing it, this is what she does in nearly all her relationships, and most of her problems stem from this. We'll return to Alicia in the next section and see what happens.

Your Options in Life Are Limited

Your family is just one of the many systems to which you belong. A system is a set of persons who have something in common. Your family has an invisible legacy in common. The country you live in also has an invisible legacy in which all its history and culture are stored. Since it's best to learn about this a little at a time, this book will help you by starting with what is most important: your family. Once that is healed, you will heal all the rest.

In order to get a feel for the size of your entanglements, you need to understand how not occupying your place in your family affects your performance in other areas of your life—at work, in your religious group, with your friends, and with your partner and children. When your family is out of order, you cannot occupy your spot in any other system to which you belong, and love and life energy will be blocked. In order to get ahead in life and fulfill your goals, you need to receive life energy. Do you now realize how big of a problem is created by leaving your place?

Let's go back to the example of Alicia, who when she should have been the little one was playing the role of an adult. When she finishes her schooling, she gets a job, and her boss quickly gives her a promotion because of her capacity to take charge of everything. Apparently, it's still a blessing to be the big one! The years go by, and Alicia keeps giving everyone everything. She feels increasingly drained. With her group of girlfriends, she is the one who listens and holds space. At work, she is responsible for a particular work area, but she is no longer given promotions, for she has reached a limit. She is also the emotional and financial support for everyone in her family of origin. She receives nothing for herself because her job is to give and give and always be the strong one.

One of the many prices she pays for all this is not having a family of her own. She doesn't see this as a problem, for she no longer has the desire to do so. Why is all this happening to her? How is she going to want to give more if she already gives so much? The problem is that she is really not free to do anything else. Her duty is to give; that's what she is known for and what makes her feel secure, though lately she has been feeling very tired. Not giving or holding space would make her feel insecure and fearful. In order to have real life options, she'd have to be little sometimes, but that possibility does not exist for her.

Occupying a role that does not belong to you leads you to miss out on life's options. To give this a number—say you have ten life options when occupying the role that is yours, but if you leave that place, your possibilities get cut down to two. You lose the freedom to choose without even realizing. It's like having to eat in the same restaurant every day when there are so many wonderful places in which to enjoy a delicious meal. How boring, right? But those who suffer from this don't even realize there are other restaurants to choose from; they only know one, and that is the one they go to. When they get bored, they think this is life. You're about to open up to infinite possibilities by getting your family in order.

How to Establish Order in a Family

Take Your Place

Taking your place is much easier than you might suppose. You simply have to be in the here and now, performing your function. It's like the "just for today" slogan for alcoholics. If you're thinking of taking on all other roles at the same time, you'll find it impossible to do, which is why there is so much stress at Christmastime when the whole family gets together. You go to festivities with your husband, your children, your parents, your siblings, your aunts and uncles, and you're playing out all your roles at the same time. You feel pulled in all directions by the different functions, and you believe you'll end up hurting someone's feelings.

In everyday life, you're with a few of your family members at a time, and as you're familiar with the elements of order (time, function, and soul weight), it's easy to determine which has priority. It just requires practice and common sense. Let me share with you a few cases so that you can see how simple this is to apply.

Paula is married and has three children. She comes to my consulting room because she's exhausted and worried about the fears her eldest daughter, Karen, is suffering from, preventing both of them from getting any sleep. What's going on with Karen? In order to get some rest, you need to relax, and you can only do that if you feel safe. Children feel safe when there are parents or other adults around they trust to take care of them.

Paula does not realize how incapable she is of creating this safe space for her children. The one who is most affected is the eldest daughter, Karen, who feels that if her mother is not going to take care of her, she has to be the one to take charge of her mother and her siblings. Why is Paula unable to provide that sense of security? Because when Paula was little, her father was violent, and she protected the family by making sure to appease her father. Paula learned to be charming so as to squelch the bouts of aggression on her father's part, storing all that angst inside.

Without realizing it, Paula is still doing this. She has a lot of anxiety that she is not recognizing, and she is being charming. Where was Paula's mother, Julia, during these early childhood experiences? Julia was there, only Paula doesn't remember her, so it's as if the mother was not there at all. Since Paula's mother, Julia, was not occupying that role, Paula stepped into it. Now Paula can't take up the role of mother to her own daughter, Karen. Paula has to decide who to be a mother to: Karen, her child, or Julia, her mother.

When you can see things with this degree of clarity, it's easy to make a decision. It's much simpler when you realize how your children are being affected. The same thing that Paula suffered in her childhood from her parents, her daughter Karen is now suffering from. Karen feels lonely even though Paula is taking care of her.

Normally, children point the finger at what needs to be ordered in the family. You cannot play out your role of father or mother if you're all tangled up being father or mother to someone else. Nor can you perform the role of partner to the person you love if you're partnered up with someone else.

This is what happened to Laura. She met Esteban when she was twenty, and they fell head over heels in love. It was one of those loves you see in movies. Things were going beautifully ... until Esteban's mother found out and launched a campaign against the relationship. The ultimatum was, "Either her or me." Why would a mother adopt that attitude? She is occupying the place of partner to her son and feels jealousy toward and competition with the person who intends to take up that spot.

The place of partner can be occupied by children, siblings, parents, and former partners. For this reason, if you want a couple relationship, make sure the spot is free for it. Leaving the place free is a prerequisite for a new person to come into your family.

Appreciate Your Lot

One indispensable ingredient for maintaining order in the family is gratitude. You've learned that a family is out of order when the members leave their place. This happens for one of two reasons: they don't like their place, or they want to take the place of another who is not doing his or her job. I find that human characteristic of wanting to occupy a different place than one's own very amusing. The normal thing is to want to be number one. I see this so often that it might even be considered a rule with very few exceptions.

When a child is asked what number he is, he would rather say "one" than "two," "three," or "the last one." When a person is asked what number of partner he or she is, that person likes to say "number one" and hates to admit that someone else is or was first. If this is the case, the person prefers to say something like, "Well, there were a few before, but they didn't get along well," which in other words means "I'm better than any other partner there might have been."

Many people get confused and try to define the exact number they occupy in their family. They think that once they know this exact number, they'll be at peace and can take up their own spot in life. But what happens when you don't have the information, and there's nobody around to give it to you?

The number you occupy within your family does not matter. What truly matters is that you take up your spot, and you can do this even without that information. But before that, you must relinquish your need to be better than the others. Wanting to be above another makes you leave your spot because the other person's spot seems more attractive to you. Comparing your spot to that of other members is what gets your system out of order.

Imagine a musician in an orchestra. He's seated in his chair, his instrument held between his hands and his score right in front of him ... yet instead of playing the piece he's meant to play, he's concentrating on what the other musicians are up to. What do you think his participation in the orchestra will be like? Is he a good element for the group? Does he create harmony or disharmony? The remedy is to be grateful for the instrument and score you were given to play.

In family systems, gratitude is the best glue for keeping you in your spot. Hurricanes, earthquakes, and storms can rage, but with a good dose of gratitude, nothing will knock you out of place. You'll navigate your family crises by maintaining order and getting love and life to flow between you and the other members of your family.

Give All Members Their Place

How do you create order when you believe you depend on another to do so? In the previous example, Esteban needs to give his mother the place of mother and Laura the place of partner. But what if his mother wants to keep playing out the role of partner, and she does not accept Laura? Each person does only his or her own part and allows others to do their own if they want to.

A powerful tool for establishing order in the family is internal images. Your internal images are mental pictures you create. In order to get your family aligned, you have to create images that are well-ordered. Once you have identified the cause of the disorder—the entanglement that has you all tied up—you will imagine what needs to be modified in order for things to flow.

If you can imagine your father and your mother being present and sustaining or supporting you, occupying their place as the adults while you occupy yours as a little child, at the level of energy this will happen, and you're going to be able to take on the role of adult for your own children. But if in your mind you're seeing your parents as little and you have to support or sustain them, you won't have energy for your own children. While reading this book, you've been creating well-ordered images that reprogram you for the healing of your family.

When members of your family are dead, it's easier to maintain well-ordered images of them. As long as family members are alive, their attitudes change, and you keep reorganizing your internal images. There's always constant movement, settlements, and disruptions. Besides, it's more difficult to create a positive picture when the person you are imagining is doing exactly the opposite in real life.

It's like a house. If it's lived in, you put it in order, and then it gets out of order. You clean up the kitchen and make the bed, and the following day, you have to do it all over again. Like cleaning the kitchen, you might think this is a never-ending job. I look at it as a fun part of life because by learning to disentangle your family entanglements, you get stronger and evolve. Every day you become a happier person. You gain in soul weight and become wiser.

Besides, it's not really like washing dishes, as the tasks are not routine. If you learn to stay in your place and give all other family members their own, those entanglements will no longer occur. However, as long as there are members in your family, the need to reshuffle will become evident within the system. This is what teaches us lessons and gives us life.

As you will have noted, it's clear when a family is out of order because there's disharmony. To reestablish order, you merely need to take your place and give everyone else the place that corresponds to that individual. This you do without having to fight anyone or educate the others.

Let's go back to the example of Laura and Esteban. What can they do about his mother, who does not want to accept Laura? Laura and Esteban can create an image in which they give the proper place to Esteban's mother and their union is blessed. They attune themselves to this picture and choose to have this experience. At the same time, they respect the way Esteban's mother wants to experience things. When they integrate a well-ordered picture within, they gain clarity about what they want to do in a practical manner.

They may decide to live close to her or not. They may avoid seeing her, thus making it easy to preserve the positive image, but this depends on them and on how strong they are. The important thing is for them to stop carrying what belongs to other members of the family. In this manner, if there is aggression, it won't touch them. They can enjoy their love by occupying their place as a couple.

When you've been out of order and stop occupying places that are not yours and only carry what corresponds to you, a deep movement takes place in your family system. Previously, there was some semblance of balance, albeit off-kilter; everyone was comfortable with and accustomed to things the way they were. As soon as changes are made, the entire family system gets rearranged. This brings benefits for everyone, but some people get irritated when things change. Regardless, welcome in the new structure that gets love to flow. Remember that you are in charge of your small part only and all others are in charge of their own.

Respect the Other

Another ingredient that is essential to preserving order in the family is respect. The members of a family feel a tug when they believe others are not occupying their place or performing their function properly. This tug can get to be so strong that it pulls them out of their spot. It's like when you're swimming in the sea and there are undercurrents of water; you think you've stayed in the same spot, but when you least expect it, the current has taken you far from where you were. This is how systemic tugs operate.

Respect is the antidote. When you feel profound respect for the manner in which all members of your family occupy their place and perform their function, you feel calm and at peace. You stop wanting to fix things for others and concentrate on your part.

Going back to the orchestra example, envision the musician sitting with his instrument held between his hands and facing his score. At that moment, he refrains from looking at all other musicians and comparing himself to them. He centers his attention on his score, prepares, and plays the instrument he has as best he can. All his energy is centered on himself and on doing his part with excellence. He compares himself to himself only and tries to do better every time.

This attitude is what we are shown in QiGong: "Serenity on the inside, respect on the outside." You need serenity within yourself in order to take your place within the family and calmly do what you are supposed to do. Respect toward others allows them to be themselves, take their own place, and perform their function without you trying to change the manner in which they do this. It is the best thing you can do for yourself.

Apply the Magui Block Method to Get Your Family In Order

Get love and life energy to flow freely between the members of your family by establishing order. During your reading of this chapter, you've identified the entanglements that create chaos in your system, and you've understood the guidelines for a well-ordered family. Now you're going to ground the work you've done and achieve an extraordinary transformation with the power of your unconscious.

Envision the orchestra again and create the following movie in your mind:

- *First scene*—Some of the musicians are milling around looking for their spot; others are seated in someone else's place. There are musicians concentrating on their score and rehearsing so they can give their best, while others are criticizing the rest of them. Some of them seem scattered, and others are aware of every little thing that is going on. Though they are all members

64

of the same orchestra, each musician experiences this differently from the rest.

- *Second scene*—The director of the orchestra arrives. He knows perfectly well which score belongs to whom, where they are to sit, and how they must play their instruments. He knows the rhythms and when each member must take part and when each must be quiet. He's willing to be the one to direct and has the power with which to do so. He is a director with a lot of experience and recognition, and the musicians are happy to belong to his orchestra. They appreciate him and respect his authority.

- *Third scene*—The musicians are in place, each with his or her own instrument and score. They're ready for the concert to begin. At the precise moment, the music starts. It is beautiful, harmonious, and in perfect order. The sound wafts in, freely inundating with life, light and love, to the body and soul of each person in the room.

Your family is now in order. To increase the healing power, start by adopting the right physical posture, as follows:

- Hold your body upright. Imagine that your head is touching the sky and that your feet are firmly and deeply grounded in the earth.

- Be centered. Your heart and mind are as clear as crystal.

- Place your hands, one over the other, on your belly button. Imagine that they connect to the space that is close to your spine, inside of your body. (If you're a woman, place the palm of your right hand on your belly button and the palm of the left hand on the back of your right hand. If you're a man, place the palm of your left hand on your belly button and the palm of the right hand on the back of your left hand.)

Next, evoke love:

- Remember your willingness to heal, and smile.
- Feel appreciation for yourself.
- Be thankful for the moment.

Finally, appreciate the power of these words :

- Repeat these phrases out loud.
- Listen to the way you say them, and repeat them until they come naturally to you.

Now, adopt the right posture, evoke love, and repeat the following out loud:

> *My family is in order.*
> *Love and life flow between its members.*
> *I occupy my place and take charge of my function.*
> *I stop occupying places that are not mine.*
> *I renounce all functions that correspond to someone else.*
> *I am happy to take my place and perform my function.*
> *My place and my function in the family are perfect for me.*
> *I am grateful for them.*
> *I feel profound respect for everyone's place and for the manner in which they perform their function.*
> *I renounce all comparisons.*
> *Serenity on the inside.*
> *Respect on the outside.*
> *My family is in order, and I appreciate it.*
> *Perfect order is maintained.*
> *Thank you.*
> *My family is in order.*
> *Perfect order is maintained.*
> *Thank you.*
> *My family is in order.*
> *Love and life flow.*
> *Thank you.*

Key #3: Take Life Energy from Your Ancestors

Thanks to the force that is life energy, you are alive and can do what you desire. It's your motor, your enthusiasm; it's what urges you on. The more you have, the better things go for you. Your strength depends on the quality of life energy that you take from your ancestors.

Why do we use the word *take* instead of *receive*? Because the intention is for you to open up to what arrives from your ancestors completely and absolutely. When you use the word *take*, what you're really saying is that you are willing to accept without condition the life energy that reaches you, such as it is, from the ancestors you have, such as they are. It is equivalent to receiving by acknowledging to yourself inside: "I'm in agreement with what my ancestors are, with what there is in my family, and with the amount of energy that reaches me, and also with the quality of it and with the information it brings. I am in agreement with all this."

It's normal for you to want to take life energy in the same way you eat a meal—picking off your plate only that which pleases you and leaving the rest behind—but it doesn't work that way. When you take, it is like breathing, not eating. When you take a breath in, you receive all the air; you cannot choose what comes in and what stays out. If the air where you live is contaminated, and you reject it by constricting and tightening, you stop breathing. You stop receiving oxygen, and your vital functions start to break down.

In order to breathe correctly, you have to inhale deeply, accepting the air just as it is. Breathing it all in is much better than not breathing—for if you don't breathe, you die, and if you breathe shallowly, you get sick. You also have to learn to eliminate the effects that contamination can generate.

When your family system seems toxic to you, you block what you take in, as if you walked into a smelly bathroom, became nauseated by it, and held your breath. It's just that you have to take in life energy to be in good shape and grow strong so that you can fulfill your goals. Likewise, the manner in which you receive from your family will be replicated in all your relationships. If you don't take from your parents, you then won't take from your partner in a healthy way, and you'll end up adversely affecting your offspring.

As you can see, this is a very important topic, and learning about it will bring many benefits to your life. You'll see magnificent changes.

How to Take Life Energy

From the point of view of family systems, parents give life and children take it. This means that children receive life through their parents, without conditions, just as it comes to them. Parents, by giving their children life, give them what they themselves are; they cannot add anything, suppress anything, or hold anything back. As such, even though parents want their children to get only the best from them, they nevertheless give them everything that is in them.

To liberate your children from something you don't wish to give them, you'll have to heal it in yourself first. If before conceiving a child, you free yourself of what limits you, you won't pass it on to the next generation, as it will no longer be a part of you. It would be wonderful for every generation to be better than the one before.

Parents give their offspring what they previously took from their own parents, and also that which, as partners, they took from each other. The more energy they take from their parents and from their partner, the more energy there will be for their offspring. To give your children the best, take a lot of life energy from your parents and your partner.

Children, in receiving life from their parents, can only take their parents just as they are. They cannot add, subtract, or reject anything. If a child rejects some traits of his or her parents and does not accept them as they are, that child then rejects the life that reaches him or her through the parents. Remember, taking is like breathing and not eating; when you receive from your parents and pick and choose what to take, as you do when you pick only what you want off your plate, you refrain from receiving life.

You cannot choose what comes to you from your parents, but you can choose how to use it. And therein lies the key! But first, you must learn to take a lot of life energy.

How to Take Lots of Life Energy

In order to take life energy fully, it is necessary to honor what is received and the person from whom it is received. To honor means to feel great respect for a person, treating him or her with dignity. To take a lot of life energy, you need to feel great respect for your parents, for your parents' parents, and for all your ancestors. The more respect you feel, the better life gets.

Why is this so? Life energy flows as if it were water. Imagine a river of crystal clear water. The movement of the water depends on the incline of the river. The steeper the incline, the more water flows more quickly and with force. If the water falls in a cascade, it comes down even faster. Feeling great respect for parents and ancestors makes life energy flow to you as if it were falling from a great cascade or waterfall—with force and abundance!

On the other hand, when you feel scorn for your parents, you feel you are better than them, and you then will set yourself above them, in a superior hierarchy. So then the incline flips, and life energy travels in the opposite direction—from you toward your parents. You set yourself up as the adult and your parents as the little ones, so you give them life energy, and they take it from you. You end up drained, and all thanks to feeling superior to them.

The way you relate to your parents determines the way you'll live your life. When you accept and acknowledge them just as they are, you receive lots of life energy. When you belittle them—no matter how justified you feel in doing so, given what you experienced with them—no life energy can flow to you. Belittling parents is belittling life. Appreciating parents is loving life.

You can only love and honor your life when you love and honor your parents. However, loving them does not mean sticking by them if they are toxic to you. What can you do if your parents take from you rather than give?

Toxic Parents and Ancestors

A toxic parent or ancestor is one who instead of nourishing progeny sucks the life energy out of them. Parents and ancestors are the ones who give life, but in this case, rather than giving, they are taking. This hurts their progeny.

How can you take life energy if your parents or ancestors are toxic? Most people who have toxic parents do one of two things: they believe everything is going to be fabulous in their life if they keep away from their parents, or they live right up against their parents, near them, in the hope of receiving something from them.   No matter whether you live far from or close to your parents, the solution lies in healing the relationship you have within. Whatever you do externally will be a reflection of what happens on the inside when you are in harmony.

The first step in solving this is to let go of the fantasies you've created in your mind. These are waylaying you. Relinquish your thoughts about having your parents change, act differently with you, or do what they would have to do to make you feel good. No longer wait for your parents to ask your forgiveness for the way they mistreated you in the past or reward you for how badly they made you suffer. When you take full responsibility for your own healing, you'll do this very quickly.

There are some who think that parents have to deserve the right to be acknowledged by their children. They think a bad father or a bad mother does not deserve recognition. What's more, they believe that if there was abuse, contempt and blame are justified. But not taking life energy from the parents becomes punishment for the child. If there was already abuse, must that child suffer from a lack of life energy as well?

There are children who refuse to accept their parents, reproaching them with the idea that what they received was inadequate or different from what they desired. So they keep waiting to receive from their parents and are unable to move toward life. This attitude forces them to stick close to their parents, without progressing and without receiving what they desire. If your parents did not give you what you needed in the past, what makes you think they'll give it to you now? The best thing you can do for yourself is to move toward life, but you can only do this if you're grateful for what you've received, though it might not be what you wanted.

Sometimes a child demands that his or her parents have certain qualities in order for them to "gain" the right to have life energy taken from them, and justifies not taking from them because of their defects.

It's as if the child is saying to the parents, "In order for you to be my parents, you have to be as I want you to be." In this manner, children substitute taking with demanding and respect with reproach.

However, when a child demands, parents lose their desire to give. It's like a waterfall that dries up, and the water no longer flows. When children are very demanding, the parents are worn out and have less patience. On the other hand, when children are caring and appreciative, the desire to give surfaces naturally.

That is why, although your parents might be toxic, you must be grateful for what there is. This attitude gets more of the good to come your way, and the bad dissolves. Gratitude and respect are the ingredients that protect you from any toxicity in the family system. The more toxic you consider your parents and ancestors to be, the more respect and gratitude you need to feel.

You're going to learn ways to connect to ancestors who have a lot of life energy for you. In the meantime, choose to change your attitude. Fill yourself up with gratitude for yourself for being who you are, even with the parents you were given.

Adoptive Parents and Ancestors

Life energy comes from the biological family and not from the foster or adoptive family. Adoptive parents and ancestors give love and care, but they do not give life. Most probably, they would have liked to have given everything to their charge and may feel resentment toward the biological parents, yet the more they respect and appreciate the biological parents, the better off their adopted children will be.

The problem is that, generally, adoptive parents consider the biological parents to be toxic for their children. Many believe they deserve to be the true parents of their adopted children, and so they exclude the biological parents. When a member of the family is excluded, the life stories get repeated. Do you think adopted children benefit from having to repeat the story of one of their biological parents?

Expand your heart and include your adopted children's biological parents and ancestors. They hold a very important place for your adopted children, as this is where their life energy comes from. You can give them a lot, but not life energy. Accept and honor where they get life from. Their invisible family legacy is from their biological family, and it tugs at them for what is beneficial or harmful to them. Acknowledge their invisible family legacy, as only in this way will you be able to help them with their challenges.

What Reasons Are There for Not Taking from Parents and Ancestors?

There are several reasons for children to either not want to take from their parents or be unable to. When there is a serious defect in the family, children are afraid of inheriting it and close themselves off, refusing to take from the father or mother who suffers from this. If the child wants to take from the father or mother but that biological parent is not available, the child is left without that part of his or her lineage. This can be extremely painful. The child needs permission to be able to take from both sets of parents.

Sometimes the mother gives a child life energy only as long as he or she does not take what comes from the father, and the father gives only if the child takes just what comes from him and rejects that coming from the mother. In such a case, the child is put in a precarious position and must make a choice.

When the flow of energy from the mother is cut off, nothing that can potentially come from the maternal ancestry is allowed in. The same thing occurs when the link to the father is cut: all that is in the father's lineage is cut off as well. The child is bereft of the possibility of taking those ancestors' life energy and remains tied to his or her family, as this energy is necessary for moving on.

Though it might seem to you that your reasons for not taking from your parents and ancestors are valid, you are the most affected party when you cut off the flow of life toward yourself. You may feel empty, angry, depressed, sick, confused, or still attached to your parents internally. You may not have a sense of life. You'll now learn how to deal with the things that prevent you from taking your parents and ancestors. You're doing it for you, not for them.

What to Do When There Is a Serious Defect in the Family

When your parents or ancestors have some defect you consider serious—such as an addiction, a mental health problem, or a physical illness—you might be afraid of inheriting it. So you close yourself off from that member of the family, and you don't want to receive what comes from that individual. However, a hidden loyalty is then generated toward the rejected person. This means that, though you might not be aware of it, you're extremely attached to this ancestor and very probably will attract into your life the defect you most fear. An example in the case of an addictive father would be for the son to become an addict or to marry an addict.

The thing is, you are already connected to your ancestors, like it or not. If you can accept this and be grateful for it, the link is open and visible. If you reject it, the link is hidden. Imagine that these connections or links are pipes through which information and life energy pass. You can't make the pipes disappear, but you can choose the manner in which they connect to you. If you welcome them, the pipes expand with life energy. If you reject them, they close off, and no life energy can come through. An underground pipe is formed, hidden from your consciousness, through which you now get the worst things about that person you do not want to connect to. You've been opened up to the bad, and you stop receiving the good.

The more life energy you have, the more efficiently you can face the defects you may inherit from your parents and ancestors. Life energy gives you strength for finding the solutions you need. So if any of your parents or ancestors has a serious defect and you're worried about inheriting it, you must adopt an intelligent and humble attitude. Accept that the information is already held in your legacy and that you're going to receive it. Surrender to the possibility of suffering from it. When you stop struggling, you can transform it.

It's like in the martial arts—you use the strength of your opponent to vanquish him when you synchronize with his movement. If you face him, the shock might knock you down. When you accept that a certain characteristic is contained in the information from your family and you surrender to it coming to you, you can use the strength it brings to achieve a positive change.

The first step is to accept that the information is coming to you and surrender. The next step is to recognize and honor all the ancestors who suffered from this. Something magical occurs when you realize how much pain your ancestors have suffered through. You stop feeling superior to them and occupy your place as the little one. Rejection is transformed into compassion, the defects are diluted, and you receive the best from your family.

Do you recall the example of the river and the waterfall? The steeper the incline of a river, the more quickly the water flows. When you feel profound respect toward your ancestors, the life energy is strong and abundant. You're the little one, they're the big ones, and you put them in a hierarchy higher up than yours. The higher the hierarchy you give to your ancestors, the less likely you are to suffer from what you're worried about. But this only works when you do it with humility—that is, by surrendering to the possibility of suffering from the same thing given the fact that you are a member of that family.

There are persons who confuse hierarchy with the value they place on someone. They believe that if they give their parents a superior hierarchy, they are accepting that they themselves are less valuable than their parents. Hierarchy has no relation to the value of a person. You and your ancestors have the same value, but you have different hierarchies. In order for life energy to flow, you need to occupy the right hierarchy. Relative to your ancestors, you are the little one; relative to your children, you are the big one.

Occupying the right hierarchy is even more important when there are serious defects that run in the family. Whoever suffers from a serious illness must be honored and respected in the proper hierarchy and for the suffering they have been through. If this does not happen, their progeny will repeat the story and the suffering. That's why there are defects in the family that are like snowballs. They roll farther and grow even larger with every generation. Here is the solution:

- Accept everything that comes to you from your family.

- Surrender to the possibility of suffering from it.

- Acknowledge and honor your ancestors, especially those who suffered from the defect you're worried about.

- Take your place in the hierarchy in the system. Remember that the little ones are free from carrying the big ones. Enjoy being the little one!

How is this done? Little by little, you're understanding the entanglements and finding the path to the solution. When all the pieces come together, you will have resolved this.

What about when you are the one suffering from a defect, and it worries you that you might pass it on to your children? Accept that it's already in your information. It's genetics, and unless you can eliminate it, you'll end up passing it on. Armed with this knowledge, you can decide what you want to do. Do you want to have children who carry this information? Assume the consequences of your decisions and recognize that there are defects in all family systems. Try to be objective about what is contained in your family.

There are people who unconsciously decide not to have children. I say *unconsciously* because "they somehow just never had kids." The real reason was a family system so loaded with defects that they did not want to bring in a child with that legacy.

So the first thing is to acknowledge what you will be passing on to your children and decide whether or not you wish to have them. You can heal yourself so that your legacy is the lightest it can possibly be—but even so, you need to surrender to the possibility that your children may inherit a defect. Remember that you can modify what's in your legacy as you pass it on to your children, but other members of the family also participate in the children's legacy. What your children receive does not depend only on you; it also depends on what comes through the family members of the partner you choose to have them with. This and many other factors affect what your children will be receiving.

So you have several options. What will you choose? Will you worry because you cannot control what your children will be receiving? Take lots of life energy from your ancestors in order to pass on the best to them? Include all the members of your family so that your children will be freed from repeating sad stories from the past? Establish order in your family so that each person can take the proper place? You now have many resources with which to heal your family.

What to Do When Parents or Ancestors Are Not Available

Children reach out to their parents to take life energy, and then they go away and move toward their own lives. This is a constant movement in which life energy is being taken and given, similar to breathing in and out. In order to be able to exhale, you first need to inhale—otherwise, what do you exhale? You also cannot inhale and exhale at the same time. Taking and giving life energy is just like that: first you take life energy from your ancestors, and then you pass it on to your progeny. You would have no energy to pass on if you did not first take it.

Envision the following scene: A mother arrives at the park where her little son is playing. The child sees her and runs toward her. The mother spreads out her arms and embraces him lovingly. The child receives the care he needs, and then, after a moment, wants to play again. The mother lets him loose so that he can run back to his friends. The child plays for a little while and then comes back to his mother for more of her attention. This is what happens when the mother is present for her son. He can keep taking from her and going out into the world as he needs to.

When children reach out to parents to take life energy, this is referred to as a *movement toward the parents*. When children direct attention to their personal interests, this is called a *movement toward life*. When children are little, their movement toward life could be to play and go to school; as adults, they could be going to work and having their own family. Children who take a lot from their parents can give a lot through their own work and children.

These movements are inhaling and exhaling of family systems. In order for children to be able to move toward life, they need to have completed their movement toward the parents. They inhale by taking life energy and exhale by moving toward their own life.

In order for a child to be able to inhale life energy, the biological family has to be available to give it. The child moves toward the parents, and the parents are available to give life energy. A father is considered available for giving when he is present and has life energy. What good is a father who is present but has no life energy, or one who has a lot to give but is not present?

There is an interrupted movement toward the parents when the child cannot reach them to take life energy. This can occur for numerous reasons, including the following:

- a newborn needs to be in an incubator

- parents die soon after childbirth

- the child or the parents need to be hospitalized

- there is a separation because of a trip

- postpartum depression

- an absorbing job

- an illness of the child or the parents

When little children need to take from parents who are not available, they feel deep pain. This pain is linked to the love they feel for their parents and can be so huge that as adults, they will not want to ever feel pain again. They will prefer to keep isolated and distant from people, protecting themselves.

What young children learn in the relationship with their parents is repeated in other intimate relationships. In this manner, an interrupted movement toward the parents in early infancy leaves a negative mark on adult relationships. Often the pain of infancy is covered over with anger or sadness. An angry or depressed adult is, at the root, a child who did not take life energy.

If children do not take from their parents, they remain tied to their parents but receive nothing. It's as if they were waiting to be given what is missing at some point. If it did not come before, it won't come now, either.

People who do not take from their parents also cannot pass much on to others. In order to give, one has to take first. Those people stay stuck, with no forward movement. They depend on what happens outside to generate a change within. On the outside, they are adults, but inside they are still little children being controlled by their parents.

Most people lack life energy because their parents and ancestors were not available, so this is considered normal. What you wish for is to heal and be in the best of shape, right? So you're going to slip out of what is considered normal and receive lots of life energy. You also want your children to receive a lot from you and manage to fulfill their desires in life. That's why you're reading this book—to be better off. This is one of the most important entanglements to disentangle.

Remember that the first step is to acknowledge the entanglement, the gravity of the problem, and what you need to do to resolve it. Focus on understanding what has been happening in your family. How have you been taking life energy from your parents and ancestors? How did your parents take it from their own parents? Were they available for you? If you have children, were you available for them?

The past only exists in your mind, and that's why you can heal it. You will create a better present and a future filled with possibilities. Imagine what it will be like when life energy is available for you and for your children.

What about Separations?

Whether their parents are still together or not, children need to take energy from both father and mother. The problem with separations is the dislike that sometimes exists between the parents, causes them to reject children who manifest features that remind them of the former partner, who they detest. These traits can show up in physical appearance, personality, and behavior. Imagine that! The couple splits up because they don't get along, and now they have a clone at home to remind them exactly of what they so hate.

When parents like each other, they are fine with children taking what comes from the other. It gives them pleasure that their child takes things from those they love, and they are joyful about the similar traits the child exhibits. The phrase "my son is just like his father" can be said with relish or with frustration.

The problem is not that the parents are separated; what affects the children is the lack of permission from one of the parents to be like the other parent. This can happen among parents who are married, divorced, or separated. It can also happen whether the parents are present or absent.

In order for children to take from their mother, they need to know that this is okay with their father. In order for children to take from their father, they need to know that this is okay with their mother. For example, when an unfaithful husband goes off with another woman and abandons his children, the mother is left behind with the children and is now in total charge of their education and upkeep. One of the sons does not do his homework, and the mother explodes in a rage. Why? Because the son is not fulfilling the expectation of his duties, and because it reminds her of the father's lack of responsibility and the infidelity she was subjected to. She sees what she hates about the father in the son.

The children of separated parents often receive the resentment toward the other parent. They receive conscious and unconscious messages like, "It's wrong for me to be like my father," "I hurt my mother if I'm like my father," "My mother gets mad if I remind her of my father." They try to override aspects of themselves to avoid having problems with the family. When one parent does not give permission to take from the other parent, children have to choose between taking from their mother or taking from their father, and they choose to take from the one they most need. If they live with the mother, they will do what she asks them to do unconsciously and will not take life energy from the father.

Sometimes, even though the parents have a good relationship and are still living together, parents may want the children to be only like themselves. So they "split" the children up—for example, the firstborn is like the father, and the second is like the mother. In this way, the firstborn takes from the father and not the mother, and the second takes from the mother and not the father.

However, children are going to be more like the parent they reject. When they don't have permission to take from one of the parents, the pipe that connects them closes off and prevents life energy from flowing through, thereby forming another pipe, one that is hidden underground, through which the worst slips by—what they were afraid of or rejected. In the end, the problem is not that a child is like one of the parents, as that is inevitable, for he or she comes from them, like it or not. The real problem is that the child stops receiving life energy and, in addition, the worst characteristics of the parents are strengthened.

If you want the best for your children, learn to be well-disposed toward the partner you chose to have that child with. Every time you see your child, repeat internally, "Every time I see you, I am reminded of the great love I have for the partner I chose to have you with," and try to remember the love there was between you and your partner when you had that child. Try to recall how much you cherished the father or the mother of your child, and accept that this was the person you chose to have children with.

Make peace with the decision you made, and love your children just as they are, with everything they receive from your side and with everything they receive from the other side. Remember, 50 percent comes from each side, and if you try to invalidate the other, your children will only get half their due. Do you want your children to be complete? Then include the father or the mother of your children and be well-disposed toward your children if or when they exhibit traits that are like the opposite parent.

How Does One Pay for Life Energy?

The gift of life comes without a price. It could be said life is priceless—nonetheless, some parents believe their children owe them a debt. Some parents even try to add to that debt by reckoning up all the caring, feeding, raising, and clothing they give to the children. I am reminded of a father who kept accounts of everything he gave his son, in the hope that the son would pay it back when he got his first job.

Most children feel indebted to their parents because they think they owe their life and everything they've been given to their mother and father. The truth is that there is a huge discrepancy between what parents give to offspring and what children give to parents, and this is where that sensation of being in debt comes from. Children, no matter how much they wish to, will never strike a balance in the relationship they have with their parents because there is no price to life.

So what is the solution? Accept the debt. You do not have to pay your parents for the life they gave you. Nor can you charge your children for it. Life is not for sale. Life is not for purchase. Life just is!

The best way to free yourself of the sensation of indebtedness is to take advantage of your life to the fullest:

- Accept that you cannot pay for the life you received.

- Stop trying to pay off an unpayable debt.

- Be grateful for your life as the gift it is.

- Enjoy it to the hilt by doing what makes you happy.

What Are the Rules Regarding Order between Parents and Offspring?

Rules for order exist so that love and life energy can flow between the members of a family. Life energy in the family must flow like water from a waterfall, up to down, from ancestors to progeny. Disorder ensues when one wants life to flow the other way around, from down to up— that is to say, from progeny to ancestors. In disorder, the progeny give life energy to their ancestors, and they have none left for their own lives.

I will share with you three real-life cases in which parents took life energy from their children:

1. Instead of being with her husband and helping to raise their children, a woman devoted her life to caring for her elderly parents.
2. A father who neglected his health now needs a kidney and asks his daughter to give him hers.
3. A son spends all his resources on extending the life of his ninety-three-year-old mother.

When parents want something from their children, how can the children refuse if, thanks to the parents, they are alive? If this is something that is harmful to them or that they don't want to do, they are stuck between a rock and a hard place. If they say yes, they go against themselves. If they say no, they feel like bad children.

This is why parents must be very vigilant about what they ask of their children, as their task is to get life to flow toward their progeny. For example, there are parents who, when they grow very old, demand that their children take care of them in a certain manner—moving into their home, taking rooms that belong to their grandchildren, being fed their favorite dishes, etc. But loving parents prepare for their old age so that their children can care for them without sacrificing their own lives or affecting the lives of their grandchildren.

The proper order is for parents to turn to their partners when they need something, or to their own parents. When they take a lot from their partner and from their parents, they give to their children in abundance and receive gratitude and recognition in exchange, but they neither need this nor do they expect it. The natural order of things is for their children to want to accompany them during their waning years, but in such a way that children can also enjoy their own lives.

The thing is, when people do not take enough from their own parents, or do not give or take what they desire in a couple relationship, they expect their children to cover their emotional needs. The children feel responsible for fulfilling what is expected of them, so they give to their parents, and the family gets out of order.

Healthy children do many loving things for their parents. They are friendly and respectful, and the attention increases as the parents get older. There is a natural order for what one needs at each stage in life. When you're a baby, you are given many more hours of attention than when you're a teenager, right? Your parents will need the same from you when they are elderly. You give them attention and perform specific tasks they have a hard time doing for themselves, but you don't give them your life energy, because you need it for your own life and for your children.

This is why you must remember the following: parents are the adults, and children are the little ones. Parents give, and children take. If your parents ask you for your life energy, look them in the eyes with wise love and say to them, "I'm sorry, Dad," or "I'm sorry, Mom."

What Are Healthy Limits Between Children and Parents?

Parents give and children take, but … everything? There are certain things that do not correspond to a child, and therefore the child must

82

not take them. Here is a list of things children must *not* take from parents:

- *Credit for what the parent has achieved.* Every person accumulates merits earned from individual effort. When children gain advantages in life due to the parents' achievements, they should receive them as a gift only. If children inherit money, a famous name, or a successful company, and then feel superior and claim these things as something they did, they are taking something for which they did not pay the price.

  What is the price that didn't get paid? The effort of having accomplished it. That child did not earn it; these are not his or her achievements. They belong to the parent. If the child enjoys advantages, he or she thanks the parent and takes it as a gift. Taking it as a right would be like stealing.

- *Guilt over something the parent did.* Every person is responsible for what he or she does, whether good or bad. Children cannot pay for something someone else has done, even if it was their father or mother.

  For example, if a father was a military man who tortured a lot of people, his son cannot compensate for the damage he inflicted, nor should the son blame his father or judge him. The son is related to the father for what the father is to *him*: the person through whom he was given life. By allowing the father to pay the consequences of the father's own actions, the son acknowledges he is free of the guilt, since he didn't take part in them.

- *The illnesses the parent suffered from.* Though it might be in the genes, every person organizes his or her mind, emotions, and body differently. Carrying an illness out of loyalty hurts the family. Children are wrong to think that if they get sick, this will diminish the parent's suffering.

- *The destinies the parent experienced.* Stories get repeated in families, especially tragic ones. That's why it's important to set a healthy limit. How to do that? By honoring each person's fate or destiny. I can assure you that parents are happiest when nobody repeats a sad fate.

- *Obligations that were not fulfilled.* Your parents' obligations are theirs while they are alive and end when they die. Children must let those obligations die along with their parents.

- *The wrongs they were subjected to.* When children try to get revenge for the wrongs a parent suffered from, they stay trapped in a cycle of violence, turning into a perpetrator or a victim. You'll learn more about this later.

When children allow parents to take charge of what belongs to the parents, they let the parents assume responsibility, and so they are fortified. If children, even in the name of love, take on responsibilities that belong to the parent, they deprive the parent of dignity and strength because, though it has the most loving of intentions, this is blind love, which is exercised out of a sense of sacrifice. This gets the family out of order. The child must learn to love wisely.

Healthy limits are a demonstration of respect toward parents and protect children so that they only take life energy from their family.

How to Be a Complete Man or Woman

Men and women are very different. This is evident in the way they think, feel, react to the world, and approach things. Both forms are vital and necessary.

When they are born, both men and women are very close to the mother, since they spent the entire gestation period in her body, and she normally is the one to care for them during the first stage of infancy. This is how the feminine is received. Later, a connection is established with the father, and the masculine is received.

The first woman in a man's life is his mother, and the first man in a woman's life is her father. This link that is formed with the parent of the opposite gender is usually very strong. However, you must relinquish it and place yourself in the sphere of the parent of your same gender in order to become a complete man or woman.

A son becomes a man by separating himself from his mother and placing himself in the sphere of his father, and a daughter becomes a woman by relinquishing the sphere of her father and aligning herself in the sphere of her mother. A man takes the masculine from his father, and a woman takes the feminine from her mother. When a man is in the sphere of his father, he is a mature and complete man who is being sustained by all the masculine strength in his system, and he respects and values women. When a woman is in the sphere of her mother, she is a mature, complete woman being sustained by all the feminine strength in her system, and she respects and values men.

That is why the best heterosexual marriage is achieved when a son who stands in the sphere of his father marries a daughter who stands in the sphere of her mother. In this way, the relationship is balanced and nourished by the energy of a healthy system. I have observed that, in general, for homosexual marriages, this issue is not a conflict, since each member is sustained by the corresponding sphere to enjoy a balanced relationship. This means that the partners change spheres to adapt to the role they play in the relationship.

If a son remains in the sphere of his mother, he will become a "mama's boy." Some of the features he may manifest include the following:

- He prefers his mother and is closer to her than to his father.
- He despises and devalues his father.
- He thinks he would have been a better husband for his mother than his father was.
- He is very male (macho) and mistreats women; or he is very insecure, like a child who cannot leave his mother's side; or a "Don Juan" (a player).
- He has a lot of girlfriends or, on the contrary, is afraid of the feminine.
- He does not see women as equals.
- He despises women.

- He is too strong or too weak.

- He is hard on his children or does not assume responsibility for having children.

- He is confused about his role as a man.

- He has a hard time establishing a stable couple relationship.

- He does not fully take from his father, and so can be depressive or lifeless.

- He has a negative unconscious similarity to the father he rejects.

If a daughter remains in the sphere of the father, she will be a "daddy's girl." Some of the characteristics she will display include the following:

- She prefers her father and is closer to him than to her mother.

- She thinks she would have been a better wife for her father than her mother was.

- She has more male friends than female.

- She speaks ill of men as partners.

- She is strong, independent, and active but finds it hard to be vulnerable.

- She has no children or is not motherly with her children.

- If she has a partner, she plays out the "masculine" role.

- She gains and loses weight, or dresses in such a way as to hide her womanly shape.

- She despises men.

- She is confused about her role as a woman.

- She feels better, more powerful, and stronger than her partner or than men in general.

- She has a hard time establishing a stable couple relationship.

- She does not fully take from her mother, and so can be depressive or lifeless.

- She has a negative unconscious similarity to the mother she rejects.

Generally, a daughter in the sphere of her father will marry a son who is in the sphere of his mother. As can be surmised, trouble ensues.

If you've just realized your partner is in the opposite sphere, this means you are too. How to resolve this? It's enough for you to place yourself in the proper sphere. How is this done? Patience! We're still in the first step of the method: understanding entanglements. Soon you'll get to the magic, when all the pieces of your family jigsaw puzzle come together and you can view the entire scene.

Are You the Same as Your Ancestors? Find Your Own Identity

They say that you are that which comes from your parents and ancestors. Does that mean you are like them? No! Every person is unique and different. Still, in order to own your own identity, you need to be at peace with everything that comes to you from your parents and ancestors.

Many people live their lives struggling to be who they are because they don't like what they see in their family. They want to prove they are different, and in this struggle, they end up disconnecting from themselves.

The foundation of what you are comes to you from your family. You must accept it, get to know it, and learn from it. When you are comfortable with what you are, thanks to everything that comes to you from your parents and ancestors, you will discover your true identity. Why? Let me give you an example to illustrate this.

What comes from your parents and ancestors is like a bottle, and your unique quality is liquid. You cannot show up without a bottle to contain you. You need what comes to you from your family in order to be here, in life, on earth. If you accept this, your bottle will be very large and solid, and you can fit a lot of liquid in it. If you reject it, you will have no bottle, and you will not be able to manifest what you are.

This makes sense, right? So make peace with your parents and ancestors and be yourself.

How to Fix Things with Your Children or Parents

This book may have reached you when you do not yet have children or when your children are very young. You will have the opportunity to apply what you're learning and prevent yourself from making some mistakes. But what if your children are already grown up? What can you do if they are resentful toward you? Is there anything you can do to remedy this? Of course there is!

When your family heals from you extending toward your ancestors, it also heals from you toward your progeny. You focus on healing your lineage moving upward, and they will naturally heal in the opposite direction. So it is possible for your relationship with your children to have a positive transformation.

Remember that we all choose for ourselves regarding our life and how we wish to experience it. You can decide how to confront your own situation, and your children will decide for themselves. Likewise, you will feel more fulfilled.

An important step in the process is to forgive yourself. You did the best you could with what you knew at the time. Now you have more resources and can do it better. Do you feel it's too late? If you're alive, there's still time.

Remember that you participate in the family legacy, and everything you heal enters it there, filling the members of your family with new and positive possibilities. If you don't see it reflected in this generation, you will in the next one. If you're no longer alive by then, you'll have the satisfaction of knowing your progeny will enjoy a family with more life energy and fewer sad stories. Is this not worth the effort?

Speaking of progeny, one of the biggest joys for parents is to be grandparents. When their children have children and they spend time with the little ones, they can enjoy the experience much more. The most natural and healthy thing in families is to pass on life energy, and this is seen through the children and grandchildren. When that is not possible because there are no children present or one does not want to have children, life is passed on through one's work. You do not need to depend on children to have a full and meaningful life. There are many other ways of feeling the accomplishment of passing on life and doing something good with what you have to give.

In general, parents whose children reject them find that rejection very painful. As time goes by, they miss the children if they don't have contact. Healthy parents need to know their children are well and happy; that's why they look for ways to establish communication and spend some time together. They are tortured by the idea that they are missing out on an opportunity to spend time with grandchildren and will feel life is getting away from them.

Why does this rejection happen? Sometimes, the partner of one of the offspring despises the in-laws and cuts the relationship off. On occasion, children prefer to move away to gain their freedom or because they don't want to be like what comes to them from their origins, or because they consider their parents to be toxic and do not want to be with them or have their children anywhere near them.

Regardless of the reason, acknowledging the pain this generates is important for the mourning process. If you are one of those who does not allow your parents to spend time with your children, please keep reading so that you can learn to view things from a different perspective. Then I'll offer some possible solutions.

I've observed that people who do this are unaware of the pain they are inflicting on their parents. They feel entitled to live life as they wish, with their own children having no contact with their grandparents. Some of these people have a problem with their own parents and try to solve it by refusing to see them. They experience this through a lens of "what you don't see won't hurt you." They think that by cutting off all contact with their parents, they will not feel any conflict either. They probably feel it is their right and that it is better for their children.

The problem is that their children are going to identify with the excluded grandparents and will end up repeating the story. So they'll have a clone of the father or the mother in their own home. This is ironic because they didn't want to see that person in the first place.

By excluding the grandparents, parents hurt their children, who are the ones they most love. They also make it more likely that their children will deny them when they are adults, because family stories repeat. They are aware of none of this while their children are young, of course.

In the meantime, what can the grandparents do? They want to enjoy their grandchildren. The first step is to acknowledge the pain this causes. The second is healing your family by using the five keys: include everyone, put things in order, take from the ancestors, balance giving and taking, and end the cycles of violence.

If you are the one preventing your children from having contact with their grandparents, acknowledge the seriousness of what you are doing and question your motives. Your parents today are not the ones you grew up with. Time changes people, often for the better. Recognize the way your parents are now and what the benefits and real risks of contact would be. At least that way, you'll be doing this with awareness.

Perhaps you consider the grandparents to be toxic for you and for your children, and you keep your physical distance for protection. There are many ways of giving them their place and honoring them while still taking care for yourself and for your children. It is essential that you include them in the family so your children will receive that life energy. Find ways of relating to them and heal the connection. Depending on the situation, you can communicate via e-mail, phone calls, video conferences, or by putting their photographs in your home. The more you honor them, the less the tragic stories get repeated.

Conquer your resistance. Protect yourself and forgive. Do it out of love for your children. They will repeat this healing with you.

Apply the Magui Block Method to Take Life Energy from Your Ancestors

You're now going to put the pieces of the puzzle together to create a well-ordered, complete picture. And then you'll do magic!

Envision the following as you continue to read:

- Your maternal grandparents take life from your great-grandparents; they take energy from one another as a couple; and they give energy to your mother. Your mother takes life energy from her siblings too.

- Your paternal grandparents take life from your great-grandparents; they take energy from one another as a couple; and they give energy to your father. Your father takes life energy from his siblings too.

- Your mother and your father take one another, and they have you. You take life energy from your mother and thank her. Now you take life energy from your father and thank him.

Imagine, feel, and visualize the way life energy flows through your family as if it were crystal clear water falling down a rapids. From your great-grandparents to your grandparents, from your grandparents to your parents, from your parents to you. The adults give, and the little ones take. The little ones grow up and become adults, and they are ready to give. So life passes from one generation to the next.

Life is passed on in joy. Life is passed on with strength. Life is passed on easily from one generation to the next. Your family is in order, and all are included. Life flows. You flow with life.

Now, adopt the right physical posture, as follows:

- Hold your body upright. Imagine that your head is touching the sky and that your feet are firmly and deeply grounded in the earth.

- Be centered. Your heart and mind are as clear as crystal.

- Place your hands, one over the other, on your belly button. Imagine that they connect to the space that is close to your spine, inside of your body. (If you're a woman, place the palm of your right hand on your belly button and the palm of the left hand on the back of your right hand. If you're a man, place the palm of your left hand on your belly button and the palm of the right hand on the back of your left hand.)

Next, evoke love:

- Remember your willingness to heal, and smile.

- Feel appreciation for yourself.

- Be thankful for the moment.

Finally, appreciate the power of these words :

- Repeat these phrases out loud.

- Listen to the way you say them, and repeat them until they come naturally to you.

Adopt the right posture, evoke love, and repeat the following out loud:

> *I honor my mother and give her her place.*
> *I honor all that comes to me from her.*
> *I take the life energy that comes to me from her and from*
> *my maternal lineage.*
> *I am in agreement with the mother I have.*
> *I appreciate what she gives me.*
> *I keep my place as the little one in regard to her.*
> *I honor my father and give him his place.*
> *I honor all that comes to me from him.*
> *I take the life energy that comes to me from him and from*
> *my paternal lineage.*
> *I am in agreement with the father I have.*
> *I appreciate what he gives me.*
> *I keep my place as the little one in regard to him.*
> *I am and I feel supported by my ancestors to move toward*
> *my life.*
> *I receive a lot from my ancestors.*
> *My ancestors are the right ones for me.*
> *I take a lot from my ancestors.*
> *I have a lot to give.*
> *This is how I feel, so it is and so I am.*
> *I am full of life energy.*
> *I take a lot of life energy and have a lot to give.*
> *My ancestors give to me and sustain me.*
> *I am sustained by my ancestors.*

> *I am encouraged to live by my ancestors.*
> *And I am grateful.*
> *I receive a lot from my ancestors.*
> *And I am grateful.*
> *My ancestors give to me and sustain me.*
> *And I am grateful.*

If you have children, add:

> *With my children, I am the adult, and they are the little*
> *ones.*
> *I give and they take.*
> *And I am honored in my place as an adult, my role of*
> *mother/father.*

If you are a woman, add:

> *I occupy my place within the sphere of the mother, with*
> *the women in the system.*
> *I am a complete woman.*

If you are a man, add:

> *I occupy my place within the sphere of the father, with the*
> *men in the system.*
> *I am a complete man.*

Key #4: Strike a Balance between What You Give and What You Take

Why do we relate to other people? This might sound very cold, but you relate to other people because they have something you want or you have something they want. If you were not interested in giving them anything or taking anything from them, you would not relate to them. Besides, in giving and taking from other people, you need to feel that you do so in a balanced fashion.

This is why when you take in your relationships and then give, and when you give and then take, you are always seeking balance. When you strike a balance, you feel good. There is a sensation of justice being served, of fairness. And so you feel free to carry on with that relationship or to end it. If there is anything more you want to give to or take from that person, you will carry on with the relationship. Once you have nothing more you want to give to or take from that person, and you are in balance, the relationship ends.

When you give or take from someone, a link is formed between the two of you. Imagine this as a tube that connects you. Every person you have an exchange with, you connect to through this tube, which can be wide or narrow. A relationship is solid when its connecting tube is wide, and it's weak when the connecting tube is narrow.

What thickens or widens the connecting tube is the exchange that flows between the persons. When there is a great exchange because the two people give and take a lot, the tube thickens. It also thickens when there is an imbalance between what one person gives and the other takes. The connecting tube thickens on the basis of the importance of the exchange. The exchange can be positive or negative, depending on the type of exchange that occurs. So there are connecting tubes of many types: pleasant or unpleasant, thick or narrow.

For a relationship to end, the connecting tube must become very narrow or disappear altogether. There are people who want to end a relationship and cannot, as there is a thick connecting tube that bonds them strongly. A relationship can only end when there is balance between what is given and what is taken. When you reach a balance with someone, the tube disappears, and you can choose to end the relationship or prolong it.

If you no longer give or take, the relationship will end. If you again give or take, the tube is formed again, and the relationship is revived by establishing exchanges that will need to be balanced. Interesting, isn't it?

How Are Relationships Balanced?

Family systems have an order, and balance can only be struck between what you give and what you take from those who are in the same hierarchy. With all others, there are ways of resolving this, which you will learn later. Let's go bit by bit so that you can integrate this well.

People in the same hierarchy as you are include the following:

- partner
- siblings (when adults)
- friends
- colleagues
- social group
- clients

In your relationship with someone who is in the same hierarchy as you, the following happens:

- When you give, you put yourself in a superior position, because you feel strong and entitled to receive afterward.

- When you take, you feel you're in an inferior position—vulnerable and with a sensation of indebtedness—for you were given something, and it's your turn to pay it back or compensate for it somehow.

The sensations of entitlement on the part of the one who gives and of indebtedness on the part of the one who takes leads to compensation, and helps relationships to become well-balanced.

For example, when a friend invites you out, you feel obligated to invite that friend out next time you meet. When you are given a birthday present by someone, you feel the need to offer a gift on theirs. If someone takes care of you while you're in hospital and that person falls ill, you feel the urge to be of assistance in his or her hour of need.

Imagine you have an inner scale on which you weigh everything you give and receive. Your internal scale tells you when it's your turn to give and when to receive. If your scale is well-calibrated, your relationships will be well-balanced.

How do you know whether or not your scale is well-calibrated?

You'll seek out people who have the same capacity as you to give and to take. It's really quite simple: just observe your close relationships and answer the question, "Is there a balance between what I'm giving and what I'm receiving?"

Take stock of your relationships and acknowledge how many of them are well-balanced. In which of them do you think you give more and in which do you take more? You normally slip into one side or the other: you either give too much or take too much. It's worth clarifying that your opinion is subjective; everything depends on the value you assign to what you give and what you take. In order to illustrate this, let me share two real-life cases.

Magdalena is a beautiful woman who places a high value on herself and believes any man would be fortunate to be with her. When she accepts an invitation out to dinner, she expects a gift and to be taken to a luxury restaurant. What does she give in exchange? Some time in her company and an entertaining conversation. If her suitor thinks along those same lines, they are in agreement. Men fight to invite her out, and she feels deserving in choosing the one with the most to offer.

Claudia is a beautiful woman, but she believes she has little to offer a man. Yet she desires to be in a couple relationship. She has a date, and her suitor brings her a gift and invites her out to a luxury restaurant. He considers she deserves all that. She feels indebted after receiving so much. At the end of the date, she invites him up to her place, and they have sex. She thinks she is doing this because she really wants to and does not realize it's out of a need to compensate.

Exchanges between people function like the laws of supply and demand: if there is a lot of something, it's not worth so much; if there is little of it, it's worth more. Magdalena believes that what she offers is unique and there are no other women like her, so she is more valuable. In assigning value to herself, she sets up exchanges in which she takes a lot. On the other hand, Claudia believes there are many women like her, and she is less valuable. By not giving herself that value, she creates exchanges in which she will receive less and less. As you can see, the value of what you give and what you take is totally subjective; it depends on what you think and on what the people who surround you think.

Without realizing it, you go about assigning points to everything you give and everything you take, and this generates the sensation of being owed or of being in debt. Just remember that you do this, as do all others as well. So what is it that creates balance in a relationship? The value each person assigns to what he or she gives and takes. If you feel it's well-balanced, you'll feel it's fair. If not, you'll feel it's unfair and will fight others to get them to give you what they owe you. If you feel there's balance but the other person does not, they'll fight you to get it.

Your relationships are in balance when there is peace—that is, when you neither owe nor are owed. You cannot change what another person does or thinks, but you can modify your exchanges as long as you have a well-calibrated scale. The first step to transforming yourself is to identify the problem.

How do you know if your scale is well-calibrated? You're going to learn how a person's life works when the scale is off, and in learning that you'll be able to see the difference. When your scale is off, you feel you owe, or you feel you are owed.

Do You Feel You Owe?

Some people feel that what they give has no value—that it is not enough and they should give more. They believe themselves to be inadequate and insufficient, and they take great pains to do better all the time. It's rare for them to match up to their own expectations. These people are the ones who are always searching and trying to improve themselves. If you identify with this, good for you! Recognizing the entanglement is the hardest part. The rest is really easy.

If you feel you owe, you'll want to give without taking. Doing it this way gives you a sensation of entitlement and of power over the other. You need this sensation in order to compensate for your perceived inadequacy and insufficiency. The sensation of giving is so pleasing that you prefer to keep it over allowing someone to give you something, as if following this motto: "I couldn't feel more indebted than I do now." If you take from that other person, you feel even more vulnerable and indebted, and this you cannot tolerate, so you prefer to give without taking and feel you are entitled somehow and have power over the other, albeit unconsciously. Giving affords you a sense of security that your current level of self-esteem does not give you.

However, if you only give without taking, over time others won't want to take from you. Everyone needs to feel there's balance. The only ones who are going to want to be by your side are those whose scale is off in the opposite direction—those who take without giving. Unwittingly, you'll surround yourself with people who are abusive.

When you give, you hold a position of power; when you take, you hold a position of vulnerability. That is why giving without taking is a hostile attitude, as you place yourself in a superior position and deny the other person equality.

Imagine that you're invited to go away for a vacation, and your friend pays for everything. During the trip, every time you try to do something nice for your friend, she refuses to receive it. She gives you a lot, but she doesn't take what you have to give. This happens all the time when you're together. How are you going to feel in the end? Would you like to experience this again? Very probably, this will be the last trip you take in which you allow your friend to invite you in this fashion.

When you are healthy, it is irritating to love someone and not be able to give them anything. It's normal to want to give when you love, but a relationship can only grow when you give *and* take. If because of the knots inside you, you refuse to take and only give, you commit an aggression against those who want to give you something too.

My paternal grandmother was a marvelous being with a generous heart. She devoted her life to giving to everyone and would be furious whenever we wanted to give her something. I don't recall ever giving her a birthday present that was received nicely. During the last years of her life, she was bedridden and had no option but to receive. I think this was a way for her to compensate for all she had given to others. And I learned how serious it is to give without taking.

Though you might prefer to give, and you feel more comfortable doing so, the need for compensation exists in all systems. If you give, you'll have to take. You'd best be advised to do this voluntarily. When you don't take, others will get angry at you because you deny them the possibility of compensation.

People who refuse to take are not obligated in any way and often cover up their low self-esteem by feeling very special or better than others. However, their life only functions at a low ebb, and as a consequence, they feel empty and unhappy. This attitude can be found among many depressed people who limit their enjoyment of life. It can also be seen among people who cannot ask for anything and live solitary lives. Some people who devote their lives to helping others do it this way, and though with the best of intentions, they knock the system off-balance.

Do You Feel You Are Owed?

In the process of balancing your relationships, it's normal to feel at times that you are owed and at other times that you owe, but there are people who live believing that everyone else owes them. They think they are entitled to take and do so without considering what others want to give them.

People who take without giving adopt an inferior position regarding the other, as if their motto is, "I can't, I have nothing, but you do, and you have to give to me." Since others have more, these people think it's others' duty to give and obligate them to do so. These individuals have handed over their personal power and believe others are more capable. This creates an obligation.

Normally, these are people who have a great need, are rarely satisfied and happy, and are very demanding. They tend to be abusive and do not appreciate what they receive. They fixate more on what they are lacking than on what they have. They might be full of sadness, fear, anger, resentment, or all of the above.

All people have had moments in which they feel just as I've described, so let's analyze what might be leading up to this. There are three reasons for you to feel you are owed: you are given less than what you give; you place a lot of value on what you give; and you feel that what others give is less valuable.

How do we resolve each of these cases? If you believe you are given less than what you give, you balance it out by giving less. If you've already given and feel that you are owed, choose to give it as a gift. When you give a gift, you don't expect anything in exchange, do you? In this way, you free yourself of the unpleasant sensation and can get on with your life, ending the relationship with those who cannot or will not give you as much as you give to them.

If the reason you feel you are owed is that you place a high value on what you give, try to see it from the point of view of the other person. It might be very valuable to you, but is that what the other person wants to receive? How is it being perceived by the other person?

I recall a very spiritual woman who was married to a practical man who liked to socialize. She believed her spirituality was a great contribution to the marriage, but he placed more value on her being a good hostess when he had guests over. What mattered to him was the good financial position he gave his wife, and what was more important to her was for him to accompany her on some of her meditation retreats.

To nourish a relationship, you have to give what the other wants to take. It might be that what you give is worth a lot, but it must please the one who receives it. So put yourself in the shoes of the other person. You'll be able to value that person from an adequate perspective and stop wasting your time.

To assign real value to what others give you, apply the same solution as the point above: empathize and put yourself in that person's place in order to acknowledge the effort being made. However, it's important for your relationships to be nourishing for you, and that can only happen if you receive what you desire and not what the other thinks might make you happy. So listen to yourself, validate your needs, and stand firm in what is important for your well-being. These attitudes will get your scale to calibrate and help you maintain healthy, well-balanced relationships.

Giving and Taking in Intimate Relationships

In intimate relationships, the exchanges are united by great love, and that is why the bond is stronger. Out of love, you give, and you do so generously without keeping count. The other also loves you and gives to you without keeping count. However, the need for balance exists in all relationships, so your inner scale will get you to feel when the situation is off-center.

When you love someone and your inner scale screams at you that there is an imbalance, you do everything in your power to remedy it.

As time goes by and no solution has worked, you seek to reassign the points you give to what matters to you. You start to play with the value of the points you assign your needs, trying to balance the scale so that the relationship can go on.

For example, Patricia knows her husband is being unfaithful, but she has convinced herself that this is not so terrible for her, creating arguments like "All men do this from time to time," "It probably won't last," and "We have so many things that are more important." Yet what is happening is serious for her given her values, and that's why she's been getting sick so often these past few months.

When you don't receive what you need in a relationship and you make it negotiable, you get sick. What does this mean? You cannot change what is important to you, though sometimes you'd like to. Convincing yourself that you like something when you really hate it is, in the end, very costly. There are people who accept unpleasant situations for so long that they get used to them, so they no longer know if they like what is happening or not. Without realizing it, they live in a state of depression, with no energy and no joy. Nor do they notice how bad off they are because they don't feel much.

This is a state of numbness in which life has no flavor. It comes from having denied what is important to you. Many do this to preserve relationships that are not nourishing because they believe this is better than nothing. But if you stay in a relationship in which you do not receive what is important to you, you refuse to accept it for life. Why? With your actions, you communicate with life, and life responds to you. The message you send by staying in that relationship is that you really want to receive what you are getting there. Then life will only send you that. If you are in an abusive relationship, life will send you more abuse. What messages do you think you are sending life with your intimate relationships?

No matter how hard you try, you cannot change what is important to you when it's vital, connected to your being, and connected to what you are. In order to grow and move on, you need to take what nourishes you. That's why I believe the best thing is to rally your strength and end all relationships that are not allowing you to take what is beneficial for you.

What about when others won't receive what they want or need to take from you? The first thing is to recognize what is really happening. Why are you not giving it to them?

Here's a real-life case: A couple has been married for over thirty years when the wife decides to stop having sex. Her husband doesn't want to end their sexual life, but he seems to have no choice in the matter. She doesn't want it, and that's final. The options he explores are: continuing in the marriage with her even without the sex; staying with her and having affairs in order to get some sex; or asking for a separation. What he chooses is to stay with her by convincing himself that sex is not all that important to him either. Who takes more? Who gives more? How is each of them going to pay for this lack of balance?

Every case is unique, and we all experience things differently. However, after many years of observing family dynamics, I've learned there is quite a high price to pay for denying your needs and vital wishes. Nobody can decide for anyone else, and only you can know whether or not something is negotiable.

Tap into your real needs and acknowledge what you like and what you dislike. Assign value to what is important. Expand your heart so that you can be more generous. Listen to yourself, and listen to the others as well. Whatever you do for yourself, do for others; and what you do for another, do for yourself.

Remember that in relationships with people of the same hierarchy, you must give and receive in equal measure. If you validate your needs and those of others, you will be able to focus on what is nourishing for everyone in the relationship. This way, you'll create relationships in which both parties win. You and the other person deserve to feel nourished in your relationship.

It's important to maintain balance in your relationships, especially intimate ones. When you give much more than the other does, you place yourself above, and it stops being a relationship of equals. This is why you must only give as much as the other is willing to give or is capable of giving. When you give more than the other is willing to give in exchange, your companion feels pressured and angry, and often leaves. Generally, the one who has less to give is the one to leave.

One of the most painful experiences in a relationship is when you realize the other can only return one part, or a little, compared to what you are giving. In a case such as this, contain your desire to give, and don't give more than the other is willing to give in response. It's possible for the other to start to give a little more of his or her own initiative. But it could also be that what that person is giving is still not enough. In this case, the relationship remains in a state of imbalance, comes to a grinding halt, or ends. Do your part and let others do theirs.

There are imbalances that are malfunctions in your inner scale, and by changing your attitude and level of generosity, and by validating what is important, they are repaired. There are imbalances that shed light on a relationship that is abusive or unsatisfactory and needs to be terminated. How do you know the difference? Calibrate your scale, and you'll know. For the moment, you're in the first step of the method. Acknowledge your entanglement, and the rest will come quickly.

How Does Balance Work Among Siblings?

In the give and take between siblings, the older one gives to the younger one. Everything one gives has been taken beforehand, and everything one takes will have to be given later on.

Suppose there are three siblings. The firstborn takes more from the parents and gives to the second and third child; the second child takes from the parents and the firstborn and gives to the third child; and the third child takes from the parents and from the firstborn and the second child. The eldest gives more, and the youngest takes more.

What is seen in many families is that, in exchange, the youngest takes care of the parents when they grow old. This is not a rule, but the one who takes more feels indebted, and this is how he or she compensates— by caring for the elderly parents. Another possibility is that the one who looks after them is the one who has the most issues pending resolution with them or the one with the most generous heart. There are many possible reasons. Understand your particular entanglement by applying the rules for striking a balance as pertains to your case.

How to Strike a Balance When You're in a Different Hierarchy

When the giving and taking is between people who are not in the same hierarchy—such as, for example, children and their parents or students and their teachers—the principles are different. There is an unsurpassed level of giving and taking between parents and their offspring; the children receive life through their parents so will always be indebted to them. It is for this reason that this connection remains, come what may.

What can you do? Accept that you cannot strike a balance with the people who are in a hierarchy superior or inferior to the one you're in. The well-ordered way is for people who are in a superior hierarchy to give and those who are in a lower hierarchy to take. It is natural for teachers to teach students and for parents to support their offspring so that children can grow up to be healthy human beings.

Give with pleasure when you are higher, and take with pleasure when you are lower. You will enjoy every experience you have and feel at peace, even if you don't strike a balance. You will get life to flow like abundant water forming a lovely waterfall. What is the key? Gratitude and respect. Remember that these are the indispensable ingredients in maintaining order in family systems.

When you find yourself in a situation in which you cannot return what you have received in a balanced fashion, be thankful. Take what you receive with love, and acknowledge the person who is giving to you. You take it as a gift and are grateful and respectful in exchange.

One additional solution is to pass on to another what you receive. In this manner, children pass on what they have received from their parents—in the first place to their own children, and if they do not have any children, in their commitments to other people. Those who see this way out stop feeling indebted and are capable of taking a lot and passing on what they have received to another.

This is valid in other areas. In any relationship in which it is not possible to strike a balance—giving in the measure in which you have taken—you still have the possibility of feeling liberated from the debt by passing on what you received to another and by being grateful. For example, my relationship with my teacher, Bert Hellinger, the creator of Family Constellations, is still present for me. I took a lot from him, so much so that I consider there is a Magui before Bert Hellinger and a Magui after Bert Hellinger. Appreciating him, respecting him, and passing on to others what I learned from him is a way of liberating myself from the sensation of indebtedness. Writing *Heal Your Family* by using what I learned from him and sharing it with many who might benefit from it gives me joy. I have taken a lot from excellent teachers, and I am passing it on to others.

Now you know: take with pleasure, be grateful and respectful, and then give to others generously. This is the key to a full and happy life.

What to Do When You Are Given or You Give Something Negative

On occasion, you cannot avoid hurting someone you love. When this happens, you feel guilty and that you deserve to be punished. When someone hurts you, you feel entitled to return the harm to that person. This is a human trait and has to do with the internal scale that seeks balance in exchanges with others.

You've learned that when you give something positive, you feel entitled to receive it in exchange, and when you are given something positive, you feel obligated to give it in return. The same thing happens when the exchange is negative. If you are given something negative, you feel entitled to return it, and when you give something negative, you feel you deserve to be punished.

Only when the two—the one who did the damage and the affected party—feel that the guilty party has received "punishment" is there the possibility of a reconciliation. There are two options for compensation: one is for the affected party to return a little less of the damage he or she received, and another—which to my way of seeing is more coherent—is for the one who caused the damage to compensate by doing something good for the affected party.

It's most likely that this comes about naturally, without your noticing. People whose inner scale is well-calibrated do this; their basic common sense tells them how to maintain healthy relationships. For example, you agree with one of your friends to go to the movies, you buy the tickets, and your friend does not arrive. How do you strike a balance? There are two options: you either return the favor, but in a small way, or you are compensated with something positive.

The ideal thing is for your friend to compensate for this mishap with something positive—for example, by inviting you out to the movies, visiting you, listening to you talk about some problem you're having, or apologizing. But if your friend does nothing in the way of compensation, what you can do is tell him it bothered you, not speak to him for a while, and not return his calls immediately. Actions like these are good examples of returning a little less damage than what was done to you. You don't have to inflict serious punishment. These are small actions that take place naturally in relationships, with the intention of setting limits and establishing the way in which you wish to be treated by others.

In an intimate relationship, when one forgives before having been compensated beforehand, a greater imbalance ensues that can destroy the exchange and the relationship. That is, forgiving helps you leave pain and anger behind, but it must be exercised once the relationship is well-balanced. For example, one member of a partnership squanders all the savings the other has saved up for them to buy the house of their dreams. Do you think that if the affected party forgives this, the one who took the money will feel better or more miserable? And will the affected party be able to carry on from here as a couple as if nothing had ever happened?

When forgiveness is dispensed swiftly, the punishment phase is skipped, and the latter is very important for balance to be struck. The punishment serves both parties: the one who caused the damage pays for the guilt, and the affected party releases anger and pain. Only in this manner will both parties be on the same level again. Forgiveness serves to turn the page and write a new chapter in their lives. If the one who did the damage is not punished in any way and is still forgiven, that individual will be placed in a much lower hierarchy than the partner and will never be at the same level. The distance will weigh heavily on both.

When your scale is well-calibrated, you know what punishment you must apply or receive, and you do this naturally. The punishment must be a logical consequence of what transpired. For example, in the cases I have seen, when infidelity is discovered, a couple separates. Afterward, they decide whether they want to come back together or not, and they take stock of the damages and the causes. Based on these, there is compensation. Each party remedies his or her part, and forgiveness arrives once the two have done their part on behalf of balance. Sometimes punishment can be as simple as profoundly regretting what was done or the sensation of guilt for the pain caused. When the punishment is sufficient, forgiveness brings the gift of a clean slate with no past charges on it.

If one of the two is the "bad guy"—the one who did the damage—and the other is the "good guy"—the one who suffered—they won't be able to start out from the same place. One will be superior to the other, and the relationship will be lost. When one party is hugely indebted to the other because of mistakes made and they are still together, even though the other feels good and victorious, in reality he or she is losing.

Remember that the party who feels inferior is the one who gets angry and leaves. This "leaving" can be at the emotional level. It's better to set a punishment than to be so good and forgive everything done to you. You will only surround yourself with people who are abusive or people who feel very badly about themselves. The most loving thing to do is to let them pay for what they have done.

Setting punishments to get back at someone or to make someone feel bad is a different thing. Negative exchanges destroy many relationships and make people unhappy. If someone does something negative to you and you return the favor, the other person will feel entitled to return something negative right back to you too. This story has no end, as everyone feels offended and entitled to get back at the other.

Forgiving someone who does something negative to you and staying in the relationship without that person offering compensation is also not a good idea, and you've seen why. The relationship will be off-kilter, and unless that person is sorry for what was done, he or she will inevitably do something else to hurt you again. So how to find the happy medium?

Let me give you another example: A wife forgets a commitment she had made with her husband. If the husband "punishes" her with a logical consequence of her actions, it might look something like one of these examples:

- The husband is upset with her for a while.

- The husband explains how he was affected by her neglect.

- The husband asks to be compensated by her doing something he enjoys, i.e., watch a movie together that he likes and she does not like so much, have her cook him a meal, etc.

If the wife acknowledges her neglect, is sorry, and wishes to compensate with something positive, she might think of one of the following:

- She offers a sincere apology.
- She compensates by giving him something he likes a lot.
- She pampers him with a delicious meal or a massage.

There are many possible solutions in family systems, and any one of these could work. Every system tries them out until the perfect balance is struck.

What would not be so adequate? For the husband to want to do the same to the wife as a way to get back at her—for example, the next time she has a commitment, he "forgets" about it. This could generate a negative exchange in which they keep hurting each other ad nauseam.

What is the conclusion? Compensate with something positive for all the negative things you give in your relationships. And if you are given something negative, do what you can to be offered positive compensation. If that is not possible, find a logical, prudent punishment. Once you are in balance, forgive. In this way, you fulfill the expectations of both love and justice, and the positive exchange can be reinstated and continue.

How to Achieve Happiness and Commitment in Your Relationships

You enrich your life to the extent that you take and you give. If you take and give little, your life functions at its minimum. On the other hand, you enjoy a full life when you take and give a lot.

The further the exchange is extended, the more the connecting tube thickens, and the stronger the link becomes. This means that a person who gives a lot and who takes a lot generates pleasant connecting tubes and stronger links to others. For this reason, if you wish to increase your list of friends, you have to take and give much more than what you have been doing.

The level of commitment is equal to the thickness of the connecting tube. When people commit, they can take and give more. On the other hand, when people want to be free, with no connecting tubes, they take and give little.

Happy people have much to give because they have taken in abundance. They are committed to connecting tubes that give them support and nourish them. The extent to which you can undertake commitment is related to your capacity to take and your willingness to give to another.

How do you learn to take in abundance? The way in which you take now has to do with the way in which you learned to do so from your parents. Nobody can give you what you must take from your parents and ancestors, and your relationship to them leaves a mark on all the connections you have with others. If you were able to take from your parents and learned to do so with pleasure, your connections to other people will be well-balanced. If you did not, your relationships will be complicated, and you will struggle to find happiness. The good thing is that you can now learn and improve.

To summarize, people who take a lot give in abundance. They are happy and willing to commit. An example of this is Mother Theresa of Calcutta, who tended to the poor, the sick, orphans, and the dying for over forty-five years while her congregation expanded throughout India and other countries in the world. Why was she able to give so much? She used to say that she took from God, and because of that, she was able to give so much, be happy, and be fully committed. The more she gave, the more she took, the happier she felt, and the more committed she was. This is how it works.

Happiness and commitment go hand in hand and are achieved by giving and taking a lot. So get on with your taking and giving in abundance.

Apply the Magui Block Method to Strike A Balance Between What You Give and What You Take

You are now going to apply the method to strike a fair balance between what you give and what you take in your relationships. During your reading, you have been able to learn the importance of having fair exchanges and of calibrating your internal scale. You might even have recognized the need to clean up your relationships, ending some of them or modifying the manner in which you give and take. The entanglements have been identified, and the path to a solution has been integrated. Now you're going to use the part that is missing to accomplish a positive change.

Start by adopting the right physical posture, as follows:

- Hold your body upright. Imagine that your head is touching the sky and that your feet are firmly and deeply grounded in the earth.

- Be centered. Your heart and mind are as clear as crystal.

- Place your hands, one over the other, on your belly button. Imagine that they connect to the space that is close to your spine, inside of your body. (If you're a woman, place the palm of your right hand on your belly button and the palm of the left hand on the back of your right hand. If you're a man, place the palm of your left hand on your belly button and the palm of the right hand on the back of your left hand.)

Next, evoke love:

- Remember your willingness to heal, and smile.
- Feel appreciation for yourself.
- Be thankful for the moment.

Finally, appreciate the power of these words :

- Repeat these phrases out loud.
- Listen to the way you say them, and repeat them until they come naturally to you.

Now, adopt the right posture, evoke love, and repeat the following out loud:

> *I strike a balance between what I give and what I take.*
> *My exchanges are fair.*
> *I take what I am given with joy and love.*

*I give to others with joy and love, such that it nourishes
    them and benefits the relationship.*
I enjoy being vulnerable and taking.
I take in abundance.
I only take what is good for me.
I take as much as I want to give.
I enjoy giving generously.
I give what the other wants to receive.
I give as much as the other wants to give to me.
I give by respecting myself and respecting the other.
I give and take in balance.
I am given to and taken from in balance.
I compensate for the negative I have given and taken.
My exchanges are fair.
There is balance between what I give and what I take.
I end all relationships that are out of balance.
My relationships are nourishing.
I take what I am given with joy and love.
I give and take in balance.
My exchanges are fair.
There is balance between what I give and what I take.
I give and take in balance.
I am in perfect balance.
I am given to and taken from in balance.
I am in perfect balance.
I am in perfect balance.
Thank you.

Key #5: Resolve Your Cycles of Violence and Find Peace

It's often difficult to see yourself as a victim or as a person who hurts others. Try to read what follows with an open mind and a soft heart. You'll learn about the theory and later will be able to ground it in practice with real-life cases. Only if you allow the information to seep in will you be able to transform yourself and resolve your cycles of violence. You'll manage this easily if you do not resist. You will gain a profound understanding of the dynamics you find yourself currently entangled in when you can see what you and others are doing in a new and different light.

How Does One Get into a Cycle of Violence?

Your relationships require balance and justice or fairness. When others cause harm, the natural thing is to want them to receive punishment for what they have done. In general, human beings tend to defend the one they consider to be weaker and needier. There is an instinct for justice that drives you to help the needy; this becomes evident after events like a tsunami, an earthquake, or some other tragedy. However, this instinct for justice that is a human quality can generate cycles of violence when out of balance.

When someone hurts you, you feel entitled to return the favor. The greater the damage you have inflicted upon you, the more entitled you feel to cause harm to the other. You want and need for that person to pay for what he or she has done, to be punished, to suffer as you have suffered, so you cause that person harm in return. The other will feel the harm you inflicted is uncalled for or is too severe. Maybe this individual feels that what he or she did was not such a big deal, or is even unaware of the damage done. Measuring the damage and the suffering is subjective. Now it's the other who feels entitled to do you harm in search of justice and balance.

You start out as a victim, having been hurt by another, and then you feel entitled to get back at that person. At that point, *you* become the perpetrator, the person who does harm. The other started out as your perpetrator and later became your victim, thereby generating a victim–perpetrator perpetrator–victim cycle in which the violence continues to increase. The following real-life case clearly illustrates how a person goes from being the perpetrator to being the victim, and the cycle of violence grows.

Candence starts to steal little by little at her place of work. One of her uncles discovers this and asks her for money. She does not have any, and her uncle threatens to tell on her. Now she has to steal more, as she feels pressured by him. When taking the money, she is found out at work and is fired. Candence begs her boss not to fire her; she apologizes, but he won't accept her apology.

The boss decides not to go to the police, because if he does, Candence would be imprisoned, and he doesn't want to go to such extremes. However, he's very angry, and when anyone speaks of her or asks after her, he says she no longer works for him because she stole from him. Candence feels offended and degraded. Being exposed in this way seems much worse than the fact that she was stealing. So she invents a story of sexual harassment and garnishes it, increasing the gravity of the accusations. She hires a lawyer who believes her and takes pity on her. Who would not believe a poor young thing trembling with fear?

As there is no evidence of the sexual harassment that presumably went on for years, they decide to sue at work, and they get compensation. The boss has now suffered from theft and false accusations, and besides that, has had to give money for something that he did not do—although he was the one who wasn't discrete and did not file a complaint regarding the theft in a timely manner. Candence stole; was threatened by her uncle and forced to steal some more; was not treated with dignity at work when the cause of her leaving was mentioned; and accused someone unjustly, obtaining more money than was her due.

Both Candence and her boss participated in a cycle of violence, exchanging the roles of victim and perpetrator. It could be said that Candence was the perpetrator and her boss the victim. But both of them took part and are responsible. The boss might have continued the cycle of violence by going after her legally and putting the case in the hands of private individuals, throwing money and energy at this, but what he chose to do was cut off the cycle of violence, file a complaint, and allow public justice to take its course. What happened afterward? Apparently nothing, but his relationship with Candence ended, and the boss no longer felt like a victim or a perpetrator.

Sometimes you get involved in other people's cycles of violence, as happened to the lawyer who defended Candence. If you have not been harmed but consider that the person or persons who suffered are not in a strong position to defend themselves, it's likely that you would feel obliged to offer protection. In any case, the victim–perpetrator perpetrator–victim cycle is the same and can grow in violence. For this reason, before getting involved in something, look into what really is going on. Sometimes the person who appears to be a victim is the perpetrator.

What Does It Mean to Be a Victim and to Be a Perpetrator?

The victim and the perpetrator are two forces or energies that form part of all family systems. They show up in the family as specific persons who participate in a story of violence.

A victim is the person who suffers harm provoked by another or by several other people, or by overwhelming forces like natural disasters or wars. This damage is inflicted either intentionally or unintentionally, and it can be physical, material, moral, or psychological. Victims not only *feel* powerless but really *are* powerless; they cannot defend themselves and are in danger because they lack the strength to successfully confront what is harming them.

You are a victim when you (or close members of your family) are in danger or suffer from harm and cannot protect yourself. You recognize you are a victim of the sensation of panic, vulnerability, feeling overwhelmed by the circumstances, and being totally dependent on the help others can give you. Victims include people who suffer from medical malpractice, theft, kidnappings, murder, rape, assaults, accidents, terrorism, wars, and losses due to natural disasters.

Perpetrators are those who commit a crime or do damage to someone else—either the person directly or the person's goods. The damage might occur as in an accident or be inflicted intentionally. Perpetrators feel strong and powerful, entitled to hurt, as if reason or justice were on their side. This person feels no sense of danger but rather feels invincible.

You are in the perpetrator mode when you feel full of rage, have no thought of consequences, explode without listening to anyone, feel your truth is the only one that exists, and are not open to anything. Perpetrators are those who steal, attack, rape, kidnap, commit crimes, assault, participate in terrorist acts, kill, or hurt others in accidents. Energies such as these can be witnessed every day in the international and local news. There are victims and perpetrators in demonstrations. A victim can become a perpetrator in an instant, and vice versa. These forces remain so united that they always arrive together.

Being honest with yourself, you will be able to acknowledge that you have experienced both forces, and in fact they are necessary when well managed. When you are in victim mode, you recognize how small you are; you humble yourself, ask for help, and are able to receive it. When you are in perpetrator mode, you feel powerful and are able to protect yourself, your loved ones, and what is yours. Sometimes you are the victim, and at other times the perpetrator, so welcome these two forces and acknowledge them in yourself.

Is Being a Victim or a Perpetrator Part of Your Destiny?

What is destiny? It's what every person comes to experience. And is it written? According to Bert Hellinger, destiny is, in great measure, predetermined through your parents, your country, and all those you coincide with. This means you are not totally free to decide, as there are hidden forces that influence your life and the actions you undertake. This sounds logical, doesn't it?

The more powerful a person is, the freer he or she is to make a decision. You can liberate yourself from victim or perpetrator mode by healing the family affairs preventing you from doing what you desire. For example, when you receive a lot of life energy from your ancestors, you have the strength and the resources you need to do whatever you want. When you are not carrying others' destiny, you can do what pertains to you. When you occupy your place in the family, you occupy your place in the world. When your exchanges are well-balanced, your relationships are healthy, and they propel you to give your best without being mistreated or mistreating others.

You have learned that every member of the family has a function and that when people do not fulfill their function, others feel the tug to do it in their stead. When victims or perpetrators from a family's past do not occupy their place or assume responsibility for their story, someone in the family will repeat it. If that someone is you, you're going to be involved unconsciously, out of blind love, in some sort of violent event.

For example, a wealthy family loses their goods in the Mexican Revolution. The grandparents are resentful and cannot accept what happened, recalling with melancholy and rage what they had that was taken from them. They are always talking about their perpetrators, and their attention is similarly focused. They do not speak of the victims. There is such pain in their recalling of what they experienced that they do not acknowledge the workers at the hacienda who were killed, the women who were stolen from and raped, and the family members who were murdered. They stay focused on the less painful parts and focus all their rage on their aggressors, not wanting to remember what they lost that is most painful to them. By doing this, they are excluding the victims.

When you exclude a member of your family, you unconsciously repeat that person's story. If you exclude a victim, you will suffer from some event in which you will be a victim. If you exclude a perpetrator, you will become one. All this will happen without you even realizing it. You do this out of blind love for your family, sacrificing yourself because you believe this is what you have to do for them.

In the case of the family that was a victim of the Mexican Revolution, several of the grandchildren lost their money in frauds or were victims of accidents and medical malpractice. Unwittingly and unconsciously, they attracted perpetrators out of loyalty to the family and repeated the story in which they would play the victim. The cycles will be repeated until they take steps to heal and resolve their cycles of violence, as you are about to resolve yours.

As you can see, victims and perpetrators fulfill a function and a destiny within family systems. When your relationship with another person makes you happy and nourishes you, you accept that person with pleasure as part of your destiny. On the other hand, when your relationship with the other person hurts you, you want to see justice done, and you want to be compensated for the damage you have been subjected to. In this case, you won't accept it as part of your destiny. Yet accepting it is an important step.

The solution is to look at the person who harmed you, acknowledge that your destinies are interwoven, perceive this person as a human being within a greater context who is united with your family system, and perceive yourself as united with your family system. In this manner, you connect to a higher power where individual differences and individual damages are compensated for. Thus you can love your destiny just as it is. This love for your destiny provides you with greatness and power because you are at peace with your life and with what you have experienced.

When you acknowledge that a connection to your family exists, you discover entanglements and can disentangle them; but if you keep thinking that everything you do is voluntary, you're denying the power that your unconscious has over you. How can you resolve this if you deny it?

That is why Bert Hellinger says that many times perpetrators are also victims—victims of what their system and their destiny dictate. However, regardless of destiny and the dictates of the system, you are responsible for your actions. Even though a perpetrator has acted out of family loyalty, he or she is responsible for all the damage done, and in order to be at peace will have to assume the guilt concerning the victims.

With this point of view, it's much easier to understand what happens in cycles of violence and what makes a person a victim or a perpetrator. You will be able to unravel your family knots and be liberated by erasing from your life script any role of victim and perpetrator. First, though, you have to know how a cycle of violence is born.

How Are Cycles of Violence Born?

The cycles of violence you are suffering from in the present have their origin in the past and in the information contained in all systems that are related to yours. Your invisible family legacy includes what has happened in all systems to which you and your family belong. There are many other systems that are related to your family that you quite possibly have not considered: for example, the country you live in, the countries of origin of your ancestors and of the partners the members of your family chose, the religions they follow, and the professions they practice.

There are family systems that have a heavy load of violence due to what their members have experienced or the systems to which they belong. For example, the invisible family legacy of a Jewish family still stores all the information on victims and perpetrators even if they did not lose a single member to the Holocaust. A Chilean family, though they live in another country, carries a systemic memory of what happened during the dictatorship of Pinochet.

It could be that your family has not experienced any tragedy; however, what has occurred in other related systems affects your system, and some members—given their individual traits—could become victims or perpetrators because of that. It's important to acknowledge the cycles of violence that are taking place around you because you're more connected to other systems than you think. Learn from the past and honor what you have experienced. Only then can it all be left behind.

How Did the First Cycle of Violence Get Started?

There are inherent strengths within the perpetrator and the victim that are helpful and natural to all human beings. These strengths help individuals function in a healthy, well-balanced manner so that they can receive help and defend themselves. Yet in spite of that, when they are too active, as we can see happening in the present, they continue to grow and expand until almost everyone becomes a perpetrator and a victim.

What can be done about this? Resolve it in the present by acknowledging the entanglements of the past. Luckily, you don't have to root out the very first cycle of violence that occurred. There are much simpler ways of breaking through.

How Are Cycles of Violence Resolved?

Cycles of violence need to be resolved in the present and in the past by acknowledging the entanglements that caused them.

Cycles of Violence in the Present

If you're experiencing a cycle of violence, it's because you're in the place of victim or perpetrator. This gets resolved by striking a balance and getting yourself out of those roles. You have to experience both forces and go from one pole to the other, experiencing both by getting to know them. By balancing the power in them in order to then arrive at your center, you'll be integrating them within you. If you are at peace inside with the opposite poles of victim and perpetrator, there will inevitably be peace outside. Let's see how you get to do this.

Follow this logic: There is no such thing as a victim without a perpetrator, and no perpetrator without a victim. One exists because of the other, and they appear on the scene at the same time. The first step is to stop perceiving one as the "good" one and the other as the "bad" one.

If you acknowledge that both carry equal weight, you will see them as also having the same amount of strength and power. So the perpetrator will stop being the big strong one, and the victim will recover personal power, leaving fear behind. It is only once you are able to view both victims and perpetrators with their dignity as equals that you will give them the place that corresponds to them, and you will stop jumping from one role to the other. In this manner, you leave behind the cycle of violence you are experiencing.

According to what I have experienced personally, when I've been the victim, the more hurt and offended I feel, the more I have needed to experience the other side—the anger, the strength, and the desire for the other to suffer too. If I allow myself to play both victim and perpetrator while connecting to all the moods that arise in the process and without excluding any of the parts or emotions, I can then find peace and close the cycle. If I reject either of the poles because I judge it inadequate, I will exclude it, and it will make its presence felt in the future.

When you've been a victim, you need to find the strength to move ahead, and you get that from the energy of the perpetrator. It's thanks to this that you can feel powerful and safe, and nobody can mess with you. I don't mean getting revenge or doing anyone any harm. It is simply that by feeling the anger, you recover the power you lost when you were victimized.

None of this substitutes or contradicts the laws or the structures of justice in the place in which you live. If someone harms another—for example, steals a woman's handbag—it is the obligation and the right of the affected party to take measures to protect and defend herself. She goes to the police, files a complaint of the theft, and does what is necessary for justice to be served. Precautionary measures are also taken to keep this from happening again, such as being on the alert and remaining in safe places. This work refers only to the internal process of reaching a place of peace with the people who have hurt you in order for you to stop repeating the cycles in which you were victim or perpetrator.

What to Do If You Are the Victim

Someone hurts you, and you turn into the victim in a cycle of violence. Now what do you do? The first step, as you already know, is to stop thinking that by being the victim, you are the good guy in the story and your perpetrator is the bad guy. The second step is to acknowledge what you experienced and assume it with dignity. When victims carry their destiny, nobody in the family will have to repeat that story.

Victims and their perpetrators are united by the same destiny. Accepting this is part of healing. You might not understand this—you might rebel against it and get angry—but healing lies in maintaining a position of humility in which the perpetrator and the victim are the opposite poles that form the whole.

The third step is allowing perpetrators to assume responsibility for, and carry, the guilt over what they have done. Oftentimes victims don't feel that perpetrators assume responsibility for what they have done, and that's why they continue feeling heavy-laden and very angry. If you don't think your perpetrator realizes what he or she has done and you are carrying this, your perpetrator will never carry it. You have to let go and leave the perpetrator on his or her own. Life will take care of putting the responsibility in his or her path; if you insist on carrying it, you affect yourself and everyone else in your family.

The fourth step is to feel the energy of the perpetrator—the will to punish that individual in order to receive compensation for what he or she has done. This is the strength you require to do what you need to do to protect yourself, defend yourself, and take the necessary legal steps. If you remain in the victim no-power mode, you are paralyzed. This is where you use the energy of the perpetrator to fill yourself with power and move on with your life.

The last step, finally, is closing the cycle and finding peace. In summary, the steps for resolving a cycle of violence in which you have been the victim are:

1. You accept that your destiny and that of your perpetrator are united. Neither person is good or bad.
2. You carry what you experienced as a victim with dignity.
3. You allow your perpetrator to carry his or her guilt.
4. You acknowledge your thirst for revenge and use it to do what you need to do to keep yourself safe and protect yourself.
5. You stand in your center.

What to Do If You Are the Perpetrator

You've hurt someone and turn into a perpetrator. How can something like this happen? Let me share some real-life cases:

- Mariano is just nineteen years old and is happy because he did really well this last semester at university. His father gives him a car as a gift, and he goes out to test-drive it with his best friends. He has little experience driving, but like many young people, he thinks he is immortal. He loses control in a curve and has an accident. He is the only one to walk away unscathed. Two of his friends die immediately, one is paralyzed, and the other suffers from a bad whiplash.

- Jorge has a girlfriend with whom he is deeply in love. They go out to a bar for some fun together, and a man can't keep his eyes off her. Jorge feels a deep rage well up in him, and he smashes a bottle on this man's head. He had been drinking, got jealous, and reacted with unrestrained violence.

- Violeta has three children and a job. Between the chores at home and her workload, she generally feels overwhelmed. When she's exhausted, she explodes in such a rage that she is verbally abusive to one of her children, saying things like, "You're so stupid," "I don't love you anymore," and "I wish you had never been born." She feels awful about it afterward, but she cannot control herself when she's in the moment.

Have you ever lost control and committed a violent act? There are people who break things, insult people, or self-harm. All these are examples of the energy of the perpetrator in action. You are the perpetrator in a cycle of violence when you've either hurt someone personally or done damage to that person's goods. The more serious the damage, the stronger the bond created with that person. You are united for life through a very thick connecting tube. This is especially so in situations in which, because of what you've done, your life will never be the same.

Perpetrators perpetrate because the energy "overtakes" them and owns them. In the moment, there is no awareness; they are driven by a powerful force that makes them feel invincible and entitled to do what they are doing without measuring the consequences. It isn't until later, when the perpetrator energy is no longer present, that they can acknowledge the gravity of what they have done.

If this has ever happened to you, acknowledge the process you lived through and accept that you and your victim are united—and that you are not the bad guy. You replicated what was in your system and did not have the strength to do things differently. The next step is in accepting your real guilt and taking responsibility for what you did.

Exactly what was it that you did? Acknowledge your part, without minimizing it and without embellishing it. Assuming your real guilt gives you power. If you make it bigger, you disempower your victim; if you make it smaller, you're permitting your victim to carry what belongs to you. Everyone must carry his or her own part of the story.

How do you know what real guilt is? Examine what happened and objectively analyze what was under your control and what was not. What was under your control is your real guilt.

For example, Mariano is responsible for reckless driving. The deaths and the harm to his friends was an accident. If he takes these deaths on his shoulders, he places himself very high up, as if he could control who lives, who dies, and who ends up badly injured. When something serious happens, often people try to bargain and believe they are allowed to decide whether someone lives or dies. They believe that if they had done something different, their loved ones would be fine and would be alive. That is why it is extremely important for you to acknowledge your real responsibility. The guilt is all about what was actually under your control. Life and death are not.

Jorge is responsible for drinking too much, for being the jealous type, for not being able to handle his rage in a healthy manner, and for hurting someone. In this case, the event served to get him to learn to handle himself differently.

Violeta's case is much like that of Jorge. If she assumes her responsibility correctly, she will be able to direct that real guilt so that she will have the power to "beat" the perpetrator energy that comes over her when she's feeling exhausted. Her children are worth that effort and deserve it. The more responsible she becomes, the more power she will have for getting herself out of the cycle.

Once you have taken responsibility for your real guilt and your victim assumes his or her pain, you can look to see if there is any compensation you might offer for what you did. Many times there is no way to pay for the damage done, so it's important to recognize that and accept what is because becoming bitter only brings with it more pain.

Imagine there was a higher purpose, something you don't understand, that led you to have the experience you just had. You needed to be the perpetrator for that person. It was something you had to live through, and you cannot change that. Ask yourself: *Is there anything I could do that would be good for all those involved?*

Once you acknowledge that nothing you do will heal the victim's pain, what can you do to make it possible for that person's present to be lighter or better? For example, if the head of a family dies in a traffic accident, the one who caused the accident might pay for the dead father's children's schooling, as they are now orphans. He cannot give back the father's life, nor can he take the father's place. Nothing would be sufficient to compensate for the lack of a father. He simply does something positive for the children and for the widow, and does it with humility.

Every perpetrator must find his or her own solution. In the case of Mariano, who feels very guilty over the death of his friends, one manner of compensation would be to keep in touch with the parents who lost their sons, if possible, in acknowledgement of the fact that he is honoring their memory. Doing nice things for those parents will show them that he recognizes the pain he caused them and is taking responsibility for what he did. It also shows he has learned his lesson and that nobody else need to die as a result of his lack of prudence behind the wheel.

Most perpetrators flee. They don't want to see or feel what they have done and try to act as if nothing happened. When a victim realizes that a perpetrator is truly sorry for what was done, it is easier for peace to be found.

In summary, the steps for resolving a cycle of violence in which you have been the perpetrator are:

1. You accept that your destiny and that of your victim are united. Neither person is good or bad.
2. You carry the real guilt and do this by taking responsibility adequately, neither more nor less.
3. You allow your victim to carry his or her pain.
4. You acknowledge your desire to punish yourself, to pay for what you have done, or to flee—but instead of doing that, you find out if there is anything that might lighten your victim's pain.
5. You stand in your center.

Once you resolve the cycle of violence you are experiencing in the present, you need to unearth the real causes—that which made you carry this energy of perpetrator or of victim. Are you ready? You can do this!

The Cycles of Violence of the Past

For you to be at peace and not respond as either a victim or a perpetrator to what you are experiencing in the present, you have to deactivate the cycles of violence that are active in your invisible family legacy.

When there are victims or perpetrators in your family's history who have been excluded, their stories will be repeated. Normally, one tends to exclude some group or other. Why? Some families recall only their perpetrators. Others center their attention on the victims. I have seen that in the case of many families. Attention is centered on the perpetrators, and they forget the victims, for it's painful for them to remember.

What happens as a consequence is that they repeat the stories and become victims themselves (they experience theft, aggression, accidents, etc.). If on the other hand, they exclude the perpetrators, they include them in their actions by becoming a potential perpetrator (they are aggressive, provoke accidents, hurt others, etc.). All this takes place without their even realizing it.

Cycles of violence get started when a member of your family is, for example, murdered or murders someone; causes serious damage or is the brunt of it; or takes part in a war. In order for an event of this nature to heal, the perpetrators—that is, the ones who murdered or caused the damage—must assume their responsibility and own the guilt over their actions. The victims have to allow the perpetrators to assume their responsibility and not carry it for them. Only by accepting the destiny of each of the parties will they rest in peace.

Peace, as Bert Hellinger explains it in his book *Peace Begins in the Soul*, is the reunification of opposites that occurs when different sides acknowledge those who are excluded; mourn for their victims and those on the other side; and grieve for the suffering they have mutually caused each other. This can only be accomplished when everyone is seen as an equal, acknowledging the qualities of the other and allowing each one to take responsibility. When you allow others to take on their guilt, you relinquish your desire to take charge of justice—that is, you renounce "punishing" others for what they have done.

Reconciliation takes place when the members of a group can see the members of the other group, formerly the enemy, and can acknowledge that deep down they are all equal. Then they can feel their own suffering *and* the suffering they inflicted on the members of the other group. When groups that oppose each other do their mourning together and cry over the damage they received and caused, they stop demanding justice be served and wanting to punish the other. They realize that prolonging the violence only brings more pain. They can now direct their attention toward a happier future; focus on solutions that benefit both sides; and respect each other's differences.

Any movement toward peace should start by including the perpetrators into the family system. When the perpetrators are treated with dignity and respect as valuable human beings, they can answer for their actions. Generally, perpetrators are punished for their actions and excluded from the community. The intention behind this is for them to be rehabilitated—in other words, for them to learn to cause no further harm and do something positive for society.

When perpetrators can see the suffering they've inflicted on their victims, they take responsibility and choose to be rehabilitated. When they do not acknowledge their victims' pain, they can spend years in prison excluded and accumulating hatred. They come out with a greater thirst for revenge, prepared to do even more damage. Besides, as long as they continue to be excluded, other members of the system will represent the perpetrators, and this will be a never-ending story. Prisons grow more densely populated every day.

By including the perpetrators in the system and giving them a worthy place as equally valuable beings, we allow them to take responsibility for their actions and no longer allow other persons to represent them. This is why a good solution would be for perpetrators who are in prison to have some sort of contact with their victims—for example, by reading letters in which those who've suffered describe their pain and how the event affected them. That would allow the perpetrators, at least some of them, to become more humanized and acknowledge the gravity of their actions. This could lead to true rehabilitation, and the cycles of violence would be resolved.

Resolve Only Your Small Part

When we are linked to our group, we do not see others as individuals but as members of another group. Instead of seeing others just as they are, we see them through the lens of all our beliefs about the group they belong to.

If someone believes that Mexicans are very generous and take naps in the afternoon, when they meet a Mexican they will immediately suppose this to be so and will not even give themselves the opportunity of getting to know what this particular Mexican is like. If an Israeli meets a Palestinian and they relate to each other through the beliefs of their respective groups, it will be difficult for them to get along, as one group will be confronting another group. If, on the other hand, they set aside their respective groups and relate to each other as individual to individual, they will be able to get to know each other, understand each other, and appreciate each other.

In the film *Letters from Iwo Jima*, there is a scene in which a group of Japanese soldiers read a letter a dead American soldier had received. In reading the contents of the letter, they are able to see the American soldier as an individual just like them. The words written by the American soldier's mother are the same words they receive in the letters from their own Japanese mothers. This enabled them to perceive the other as an equal, fighting on a different side out of loyalty for his country. They acknowledged the American mother's pain, their own pain, and the pain of the American soldier.

This is why one of the first steps in achieving peace and a resolution to your cycles of violence is for you to be able to disconnect from the groups to which you belong and see others merely as individuals. By seeing others this way, you can acknowledge their pain and losses. You can also allow them to assume responsibility for the actions they took individually and not for what their group did. When individuals from different groups can do this, a reconciliation can take place that leads to peace. Every individual must do his or her small part.

If you stop carrying everything contained in the groups to which you belong and carry only your own load, you will heal your part, which is the only part you can heal anyway. You will introduce this information as a new possibility into your invisible family legacy, and it will be accessible to all the members of your family. Once many people get started doing this—carrying only their own small part and resolving their issues—the cycles of violence will cease to exist.

How to Be at Peace with Yourself

There is one other necessary aspect for achieving peace: coming to terms with yourself—with what you are. This reconciliation starts in your soul when you open up to all that you are. When you realize that you are much better off if you open up and receive all that life has in store for you, you fill yourself up with life energy and function very well.

Life energy comes to you through your parents. You honor your parents and all your ancestors by receiving with appreciation and humility what comes to you from them, so life energy flows toward you. The more humbly you honor them, the more you receive from your ancestors. It's like a great waterfall of luminous water: the steeper the incline, the stronger the force of the water as it flows toward you.

If you believe your ancestors don't have much to give you or that you are better than them, the incline flips, and the water has to move upward to reach you. As you may surmise, it will not reach you at all. When you place yourself above your ancestors, believing you are better than them, not only does the flow of life get cut off, but you also carry the unresolved issues in the system.

For example, if a great grandfather participated in a war and killed people without acknowledging his victims or taking responsibility for his actions, his great grandchild will carry this and possibly repeat the pattern by turning into a victim. The first step in reaching peace is to be humble and take from your parents and ancestors. That is to say, acknowledge that:

- Life energy comes to you through your ancestors.

- What you are comes from them, and you need to receive it from them.

- You would not be here nor would you be who you are without them coming first and being what they are or were.

THIS WILL HELP YOU BE aligned with your story and with the story of the system. Then you can:

- Open up and take the life energy that comes from all your ancestors.

- Be at peace with what is contained in your family system and, as a consequence of that, with what you are.

By being in sync with your parents, with your place of origin, and with your destiny—and by occupying the place that corresponds to you—you are strong. By acknowledging and accepting all that you are, you gain harmony and can be at peace with yourself.

How to Be at Peace with Others

Every person is the way he or she is because of the parents and ancestors that individual has been given. Every person is different because he or she comes from different parents, a different culture, religion, race, and language. However, essentially, all people are equal. They are equal because in order to receive life energy, they have to accept their parents and the groups they come from such as they are. Energy from the same source flows through every person, though the channel through which it comes is very different.

Your challenge is to appreciate and respect differences in race, language, culture, and religion, and acknowledge that all have the same value. This might seem easy when you think of someone whose customs and language are very different from yours but whose values are similar. When people from different groups (such as country, religion, language) have similar interests or values, this brings them together. The differences dissolve, and they form a group. For example, people from different parts of the world unite their efforts to care for the planet. These people, despite the differences due to their origins, focus on one common interest; they center on their goal and contribute their resources to obtain the best results.

What about when values and interests are so different that they oppose each other in some aspects? The challenge is much greater then.

How do you treat someone who was a perpetrator? Let's suppose you are not going to be hurt by them but that this refers to the internal attitude you have regarding this person. Acknowledge the other as a person of equal value and treat him or her with respect and dignity. If you place yourself above this person, you carry what does not belong to you (such as that individual's guilt, illness, obligation, or responsibility). If you place yourself below this person, you will be afraid and will be in danger. Look at this person and recognize the strength he or she has to carry his or her guilt. The message is:

- "You are powerful, capable, and responsible. You take full charge of what you have done."

- "I am powerful, capable, and responsible. I will protect myself from you if necessary."

And what is the best way to treat a victim? The most important thing is not to be afraid of that person's pain. You are not the perpetrator, so what happened is not your fault. You don't have to fix that person's life or feel pity, either. That would hurt that individual because it's disempowering.

What is most helpful for victims is to connect to their confidence, not their pain. If you see such people as "broken," you weaken them. On the other hand, if you see them as strong and capable of successfully surviving a difficult experience, and you can feel respect for them, they will be able to carry their story with dignity and get over it.

So the solution is to acknowledge your value and the value of the other; appreciate the differences by accepting that people are the way they are because of their origins; and be at peace with what you are and with what others are. See every person as an individual disconnected from a group (such as country, religion, race) in order to liberate that part, and then connect people to their ancestors so they may understand their origins. You do the same for yourself.

You will find peace by relating in this way to others. You will create a sense of community, and you will honor what every person is. Conflicts will continue to exist, as they are part of life and the process of growing. However, you'll confront them by seeking to learn from the differences. By acknowledging that you and others are worthy of respect, you enable the connection to a humanity at peace.

You look at yourself with respect, and you look at the other with respect. Respect on the inside, serenity on the outside. You are now at peace, and the cycles of violence have been resolved.

Apply the Magui Block Method to Resolve Your Cycles of Violence and Be at Peace

Are you ready to apply the method? Resolving cycles of violence is difficult work and intense, but you are now prepared to leave them behind. If you do what follows, you will help by doing your small part.

First, adopt the right physical posture, as follows:

- Hold your body upright. Imagine that your head is touching the sky and that your feet are firmly and deeply grounded in the earth.

- Be centered. Your heart and mind are as clear as crystal.

- Place your hands, one over the other, on your belly button. Imagine that they connect to the space that is close to your spine, inside of your body. (If you're a woman, place the palm of your right hand on your belly button and the palm of the left hand on the back of your right hand. If you're a man, place the palm of your left hand on your belly button and the palm of the right hand on the back of your left hand.)

Next, evoke love:

- Remember your willingness to heal, and smile.

- Feel appreciation for yourself.

- Be thankful for the moment.

Finally, appreciate the power of these words :

- Repeat these phrases out loud.

- Listen to the way you say them, and repeat them until they come naturally to you.

Now, adopt the right posture, evoke love, and repeat the following out loud:

> *I resolve my cycles of violence.*
> *I choose to be at peace.*
> *I recognize when I am a victim.*
> *I recognize when I am a perpetrator.*
> *I am at peace with my lot.*
> *I accept my story.*
> *I rewrite my destiny.*
> *I stop being a victim.*
> *I stop being a perpetrator.*
> *I identify the cycles of violence from the past.*
> *I modify my invisible family legacy.*
> *The perpetrators and the victims in my system are at peace.*
> *The victims accept what they experienced, and they carry their load and their pain with dignity.*
> *The perpetrators acknowledge the pain they inflicted.*
> *The perpetrators assume responsibility for their actions and compensate for the suffering they inflicted on their victims.*
> *The victims look at their perpetrators and are at peace.*
> *The perpetrators look at their victims and are at peace.*
> *I resolve my part.*
> *I am at peace with who I am.*
> *I am at peace with my origins.*
> *I am at peace with my parents.*
> *I am at peace with my ancestors.*
> *I am at peace with my place of origin.*
> *I am at peace with my destiny.*
> *I occupy the place that corresponds to me, and I am at peace.*
> *I am at peace with others.*
> *I am at peace with my victims.*
> *I am at peace with my perpetrators.*

I relate to all persons as individuals, disconnecting them from their group and connecting them to their ancestors.

I am only an individual. I acknowledge all the groups I belong to, but I disconnect from them and link up to my ancestors, filling up with life.

I identify the cycles of violence that are activated and resolve them.

I resolve my cycles of violence.

I choose to be at peace.

My destiny has been rewritten.

I stop being a victim.

I stop being a perpetrator.

My invisible family legacy has been modified.

The perpetrators and the victims in my system are at peace.

The victims and the perpetrators are at peace.

The victims and the perpetrators are at peace.

The victims and the perpetrators are at peace.

I am at peace.

I am at peace with myself.

I am at peace with others.

The cycles of violence have been resolved.

I am at peace.

Chapter 4

The Price of Healing

I N ORDER TO ACCOMPLISH WHAT you desire, you need to be willing to pay the price for it. The price you pay for healing depends on the effort involved in acquiring the healing. The path to healing is different for every person, in accordance with family entanglements and capacity to change. The price you pay to heal your family includes breaking the family rules, assuming the guilt over being different, and accepting your destiny and that of every person.

This will lead you to find wise solutions that transform the manner in which you relate to yourself, your family, and all that surrounds you.

Break the Family Rules

In Mexico, it is said that children are born with a sandwich under their arm—meaning that when a new child arrives in the family, that child comes blessed with abundance and will provide the food that is lacking. Having worked with families for many years, I can vouch for the fact that children are indeed born with something under their arm: their family regulations.

Family Regulations

All members of a family share the same invisible family legacy, which includes their set of family rules. These are regulations that contain all the "rules of the game"—that is, all the beliefs in the family about how life works and how it must be experienced. Examples include what is expected of the women, what is expected of the men, and in fact, what is expected of every party. You follow those regulations without even realizing it.

It would be much simpler if what was expected of you were handed to you in written form; then you could study it and choose what you like and what you prefer to do in your own way. If it pointed out the consequences of not following the rules, you could calculate the cost–benefit of breaking them. However, the family regulations are unconscious. You are born with them. They are part of you, but you don't know them. If life is a journey, your family regulations are a heavy book that you carry in your baggage, lugging it around with you wherever you go. It leads you to take different paths than those your heart might choose.

Every group to which you belong also has its own regulations. For example, you have a set of regulations on your mother's side and another set of regulations on your father's side. There are regulations on account of your gender and others on account of the religion you follow. Every system has regulations composed of several mini-regulations, and the rules contained within often oppose each other.

Let me share my case. On my father's side, the family regulations tell me the following:

- Take the greatest advantage of everything.

- Fight to get what you want. Do whatever it takes. Scream, struggle, never give up.

- Stand out. Be unique. Be original.

- Break the rules, and do things your way. If you can go against the current, do so.

- Don't rest—there's lots to do.

- You can do anything if you try hard enough. You are unlimited.

On my mother's side, the family regulations tell me:

- Don't draw attention to yourself, and don't bother anyone else with your needs.

- Be normal. Form part of the group.

- Follow the rules. Behave and do what is expected of you.

- Be measured and moderate.

- Comply, and your efforts will be acknowledged. Avoid being too ambitious.

- Accept that there are things that are too hard for you and that you cannot do. Recognize your limits.

Can you imagine what it has been like for me to put these two sets of regulations together and make decisions about how to live my life? If you also add my other regulations—for example, the ones that have to do with being a Mexican woman of my generation and the ones I share with successful professional women—what goes on inside me is quite complex! One set of regulations tells me, "Give your best and succeed. You can do anything you set your mind to." The other says, "Don't even think of being more successful than your mate. No man will put up with that, and you'll end up alone. You'd better sacrifice your profession for the sake of your family. You can't have both."

Is this happening to you too? You zigzag through life without understanding why you take one little step forward and several back. When some regulations drive you in one direction and others in the opposite direction, you end up pretty confused and frustrated with yourself. But under the circumstances, this is normal, isn't it? That's why part of the price you pay for healing is to break your family regulations, which include all the mini-regulations that make it up. And what ties you to your regulations is family loyalty.

Family Loyalties

Family loyalty is like a tie that binds you to one or several members of your family and obligates you to do what you think will make them happy. You need these ties, otherwise you'd feel lost. All human beings need to feel they are part of something—a family, a group, a system. Being part of something larger than you gives you the sensation of belonging and makes you feel protected and safe.

According to Bert Hellinger, in order to feel they belong, people are willing to do anything—even get sick or die. He says that the need to belong is the most important of all needs and that human beings sacrifice all other needs in the name of this one. For that reason, following the system's rules seems unavoidable. You have to keep following the rules if you want to belong. If you break the rules, you stop belonging, and the ties are cut. You cannot risk ending up without a group.

Imagine that every person is like a helium balloon. The balloon needs to be tethered to something big and heavy in order to remain on the earth. No longer belonging to your group is like being a balloon lost in space, with no direction and no structure. Family loyalties tie you down on the one hand, and on the other provide you with containment. You need them so as to not get lost. That's why cutting the ties to the groups you belong to is not a healthy option. To do this will leave you worse off than before.

If you think your group is toxic for you and this is why you want to cut the ties, you're going to create hidden tubes and receive the worst of what there is. Having ties to the groups you belong to is part of your human experience. If you accept them, you receive the containment you need, and you'll be able to do what you want. The solution is to lengthen the ties—that is, stretch the cords or make them longer. In this way, you broaden your scope of movement without getting lost.

Imagine a beautiful baby girl who is just starting to walk. She is learning to go out into the world. Her house is surrounded by a huge piece of land. Her parents want the best for her, and that's why they tie a cord around her, so that she can explore but only go a certain distance. Within that distance is all this baby can handle, according to what her parents think.

The baby sometimes struggles with the cord and wants to remove it. She feels trapped and wishes she could explore at her own rhythm. Sometimes she wants to go much farther, but the cord won't let her, so she cries, throws a tantrum, and gets all tangled up with the cord. Instead of the cord lengthening, it gets shorter from so many knots.

As the baby grows, she learns to speak her parents' language and stops throwing tantrums. Now, several things can happen. She may lose interest in investigating what lies beyond; why move away from what she knows if she has everything she needs here? Or it may be that her curiosity is still present and gives her a motive for exploring, so she tries to move away from the limited space her family exists in.

She can do this by struggling with the cords, trying to stretch them, and battling a great deal. The cords are like springs; you stretch them and it seems you are moving ahead, though not without difficulty, but the moment comes when the pressure is such that you are thrown right back to the place where you began. Alternatively, she can get permission to do what she desires. When she gets permission, the cord is lengthened.

Though at times it doesn't seem to be the case, your family wants what's best for you. This is difficult to believe when your parents have been absent or are the kind of parents who disrespectfully interfere in the lives of their adult children. It may seem impossible to believe when you have been mistreated and abused. But let me explain what happens: parents do what they know to do with their children, and so they repeat the same negative behavior from one generation to the next. This happens because they act out of blind love, unconsciously, thinking this is best for the family. As such, the way they treat you is their way of loving the family system.

Parents do not know what is best for a child, but often they think they do. The important thing is for you to get permission to do what you want, regardless of the way you were treated by your parents. In order to be given permission, first you have to identify the member of the family who has to give it to you. Every cord is sustained by one or several members of your family. These are the ones you need to ask permission of. When you humbly ask the right ancestor for permission, you are given permission, and the cord is lengthened.

How do you know who the right ancestor is? That's easy. You only have to ask yourself, *Who likes me to behave in this way? Whose rule is this?* And you will know immediately. Imagine this ancestor and say: "Please, I'd like to do this differently now. I need to do this my way." When your ancestor looks at you as you ask for permission with love and humility, he or she will smile and let you, mainly because your ancestor knows it's for your own good. Your ancestors want the best for you because they love you. And so it is!

In this way, you've stopped being a baby throwing tantrums or a little child who doesn't want to leave home. You've turned into a young adult, brave and powerful, with an urge to explore what lies beyond what you've always known. Create an image in which you share your dreams with the members of your family who are enthusiastic about your urge to grow and improve yourself. You'll receive their blessings and move toward your life fully supported by your family. Now the cords of loyalty propel you with wise love toward what you desire. Your ancestors give you freedom, and they'll protect you.

Create Your Own Set of Regulations

To create your own set of regulations, you have to be willing to break the rules that exist in other sets. The first step is to dare to question the rules so as to know which to preserve and which not to. This is like cleaning out your closet and removing the garments you don't like. How do you do this? You try on each garment and decide which stays and which goes, based on what you want to wear now, being the person you are in the present.

When you break a rule, you feel your sense of belonging is endangered, and this is real. You can lose your place in the group depending on the rules you break, and you have to be willing to do this as your price for healing. You'll never not belong to your family, even if you were to die. However, you can be excluded—that is, they can deny you your equality and your honor, and behave as if you do not exist. Anybody would find this very painful.

You can only have the strength and courage to run that risk when you receive support from other groups. If you're going to break a rule in your family, you need to be part of other systems that will give you love and support you. If your family is your only source of support, you cannot break family rules because you'll be too vulnerable. So, to dare to break your family's rules, you not only have to be willing, but you also have to have the support of other groups.

Next, you have to clean up the rules and preserve only the ones that sit well with you and are aligned with what you want to achieve. You'll take the rules that serve you from every group you belong to. It's like going to different shopping malls to do some shopping. Every mall is a system, and you go around choosing the rules you like out of each one. This is how you create your own set of regulations—only you are being supervised throughout this entire process by your ancestors. You inherited these rules from them, and some will be alarmed when you want to throw the rules out and take on new and different ones.

Just imagine! It's like going shopping with a great aunt who is very demanding and whose ideas about what you should wear are totally fixed. She gets hysterical when you try on clothes she doesn't like. Luckily, there are many ancestors in your family, and you can choose who you want to go shopping with.

Every ancestor sees things differently. Fortunately, most of your ancestors love it when you explain to them why you want to create your own set of rules and ask for their blessings. They will accompany you in your process of choosing, lovingly and with great patience, for they adore you. You didn't know it, but you are the favorite in the family.

However, there are exceptions to everything, and when you confront an authoritarian ancestor who wants you to keep the rules just as they are, you will have to apologize for doing things your way. It's like when an adult son falls in love and chooses to marry someone his parents don't approve of. He tells them what he desires and asks for their blessing. He speaks of the virtues of the partner he has chosen, but he is willing to marry her regardless of his parents' opinion. This is how you're going to do this, and you will create your own set of rules made to your specifications.

In summary, the steps for creating your own set of regulations are:

1. You break the rules in your family by being 100 percent determined and having the support of other groups.

2. You create your rules by acknowledging what you want.
3. You ask permission of your ancestors.
4. In the few cases in which they do not give their permission, you say, "I'm sorry," and proceed anyway.
5. You thank the ancestors who bless you, and you proceed.

In order to be able to apply these steps to your life, you need to choose the ancestor or ancestors who will accompany you in your process of creating your personal set of regulations.

Remember, the shopping analogy. The experience will be completely different depending on the ancestor you choose to accompany you. Will you choose the one who complains about everything and doesn't like anything you do; the critical one who will fill you up with judgments; the one who is sick and exhausted and whom you have to take care of so that he or she does not have a heart attack; the one who rejects all things new and expects you to do things the "old-fashioned way"; the one who is afraid and has panic attacks every time you do something unexpected; a grumpy one who is angry at everything and everyone; or an authoritarian controlling one who wants you to do things his or her way or else? Or will it be an ancestor who accompanies you joyfully and in a good mood; is loving and offers intelligent advice, and whose presence brings you tranquility and peace; is powerful, wise, daring, brave, honest, and humble out of knowing he or she does not know everything; is likeable and also friendly, pampering, and generous; or is capable of fighting for you and for what matters?

Using the power of your mind and your intention, find ancestors to accompany you who have the traits that are best for you. If the ones you know of are not what you believe to be best for you, review the "inventory" of your ancestors. Keep going up, generation after generation, using your imagination, until you find the ones closest to the top and the source of life, where the best and wisest of them all hang out. From among these ancestors, choose the one who will accompany you throughout this healing process. Every ancestor who accompanies you has something special to give you—something you are lacking—and will give it to you with love.

Envision these ancestors as clearly as you need. They will help and support you throughout the process of creating your own set of regulations—those that are best for you and contain the rules that guide you toward reaching your goals. With the help of these ancestors, you will unravel all those knots and lengthen the cords that give you protection and space in which to grow, giving you the freedom you need. The right ancestors for you—the ones who are happy, loving, and wise—will accompany you from now on.

Real-Life Cases

- Nora is thirty-two years old and in charge of an administrative area of the company she works for. She's had the same boyfriend for seven years but does not know if she wants to get married or keep growing professionally. What should she do?

- Hector is a fifty-year-old divorcee. He has two children, a boy of thirteen and a girl of sixteen. He got his "second wind," and in the past three years, he has had three girlfriends, each one younger than the previous one. He feels alive and proud of having such beautiful women by his side. He finds it a grind to have to take his children on weekends, and he'd like to rid himself of this responsibility.

- Beatriz devoted herself to her children after getting married, but they've grown up and left home to live their own lives. She feels empty and no longer has anything in common with her husband. She doesn't know how to carry on from here.

- Pedro is studying for a career that bores him, but he doesn't really know what he'd like. Every semester, he gets more depressed and confused. If he leaves school, his family will be very disappointed in him. To deal with the pressure, he gets drunk whenever he can.

All of these individuals are living out their lives according to their family regulations, but they're not doing what they really want to do and are unhappy. Family loyalty directs you as if you were a puppet. You think you're making your own decisions, but you're not. You do what you think is right, and when you feel awful, you don't understand why.

Let's recall the steps for healing:

1. Break the rules in your family regulations.
2. Create your own rules.
3. Have the support and blessings of your ancestors.
4. If there is anyone who disapproves of what you are doing, say "I'm sorry" and proceed.
5. Be grateful and move forward.

Now, you'll see how all this is applied in each case.

Nora acknowledges the rules in her family and realizes that for her to do what she wants, she has to break the following rules:

- "A wife does what her husband wants."

- "A mother devotes herself completely to her children."

- "To be a good mother, you have to sacrifice everything for your family."

- "A woman is free until she gets married."

- "Women must be submissive and obedient."

In drawing up the list of what Nora believes in terms of what married life would be like, she realizes that she has many more reasons for not getting married than advantages in doing so. Only these reasons are not real; they have more to do with what she believes her life as a wife and mother would be like. She learned this from the way it worked with the families in her system.

To create a different future, she needs to clean out her set of beliefs. She needs to discard what no longer serves her and integrate into her set of regulations those that do, such as the following:

- "A wife is happy and does what she likes, supported by her husband."

- "A mother receives huge joys and satisfaction from having children".

- "To be a good mother, you have to do what you like to do as well."

- "A woman is free, whether married or single."

- "Powerful women attract powerful men, and they relate to each other as equals."

Nora now has two lists, one belonging to the old regulations with the rules that no longer serve her, and a new, more personal list of regulations that are the ones she wants from now on.

With her new list, she convenes with her ancestors, envisioning them as she needs them to be—loving, wise, and powerful—and notes that there are maybe both women and men among them. If any ancestor is not in agreement with her new rules, she places that ancestor next to some other ancestors in a superior hierarchy, which gets that individual to rectify his or her position. The objective is for this to be the best thing for *her*. Finally, all her ancestors are happy about the changes she is making. Nora performs a sacred ceremony, burning her old set of regulations down to mere ashes. Now the new set is current. Her ancestors are joyful. Nora thanks them, and they celebrate.

Hector, Beatriz, and Pedro do the same as Nora with their regulations. How do they identify which rules need to be discarded? By observing what is happening to them that they'd like to change. Similarly, acknowledge the rules you must discard, as they are directing your life in the opposite direction of where you want to be. Ask yourself: What do I think drives me to do things I don't like?

Some of the rules Hector needs to discard are:

- "Family is a drag."

- "Children are a huge responsibility, and I find them overwhelming."

- "When you have no family, you can do whatever you want."

- "The family doesn't let you be happy."

- "Getting married and having children is like being in prison."
- "A man's worth is shown by the woman who walks by his side."
- "The younger a woman is, the better."
- "A man's value lies in how much money he has, and a woman's value lies in her beauty."
- "Children are a nuisance."

And the ones he chooses for his new set of regulations are:

- "Family nourishes me."
- "Children are a joy, and I have fun sharing with them."
- "When you have a family of your own, you grow up and learn to be generous."
- "Family contributes happiness to your life."
- "Getting married and having children is a blessing."
- "A man is valuable and chooses a valuable woman to be his mate."
- "The wiser a woman is, the better."
- "A man is worthy regardless of how much money he makes, and a woman is much more than her beauty."
- "Children are a source of joy, and they rejuvenate me."

The rules in Beatriz's family regulations are:

- "Children are any woman's reason for living."
- "Marriage dies off with the passing of time."

And the ones she is integrating into her personal regulations so she'll be happy are the following:

- "A woman has many reasons for living besides having children."

- "Marriage is renewed with the passing of time."
- "Every day I find more things to enjoy about life."
- "I love initiating new stages and easily let go of the old."

Pedro recognizes that he doesn't do what he likes because of these rules in his family regulations:

- "I have to be the son that my parents desire."
- "A good future is only achieved by studying [the career I chose]."
- "Men don't talk about how they feel."
- "I have to be strong and put up with things."
- "Art is not a profession."
- "Artists starve to death."
- "The traditional professions are the ones that count. The others don't exist."
- "As long as I fulfill my obligations, how I feel does not matter."
- "Deny what you feel, even if it has to be through drinking."

So Pedro creates a new set of regulations with the following rules:

- "Parents who love their children prefer for them to be happy."
- "A good future is achieved if I study what I like."
- "It's better for me to do what I like than to do what my parents like."
- "Men also have feelings and need to express them."
- "I'm strong, and I am even stronger when I no longer just put up with things."
- "Art is a profession."
- "There are successful, prosperous artists."
- "There are many professions, and I choose the one I most like."

- "I am better at fulfilling my obligations when I feel good."

- "Express how you feel without the need to get drunk."

Hector, Beatriz, and Pedro perform their ceremony. Their old set of regulations turns to ashes, and their lives start to function using their new set of rules. Their ancestors celebrate in joy. Are you ready to party with yours?

Put Your New Rules into Practice

Now it's your turn. Acknowledge what you want to change. Choose something concrete—an area of your life that is not working perfectly, something you know could be better than it is. Ready?

Take a pen to paper and ask yourself, *What am I thinking that has me experiencing this?* Get outside yourself and observe the facts as if you were watching someone else. Describe the rules that make you live your life this way. Draw up your list.

Are you done? Have you included everything? Great. You now have the rules you need to discard.

The next thing is for you to create your personal set of regulations—the one that contains the rules you need for living life as you would like to. Ask yourself, *What do I need to be thinking in order to do what I want to do? What do I need to believe to achieve what I want?*

By answering these questions, you are drawing up your list of new rules. These will be your personal regulations, which will guide your life from now on.

You have two lists, one consisting of the old rules that you're going to discard or burn, and another that you're going to preserve and that will become your new set of regulations. Now comes the fun part: the party!

Invoke your ancestors, and invite them to the ceremony. You are achieving all this by using the power of your mind and your imagination. Your ancestors are just the way you need them to be: cheerful, loving, wise, powerful, and calm. There are women and men among them.

If there are ancestors who are angry, sad, or afraid because they're not in agreement with what you're going to do, surround them with ancestors of a higher hierarchy who can get them to calm down. Now all your ancestors are happy about the changes you're making. All of them want the best for you.

Start your sacred ceremony. Burn your old regulations, the ones that have guided your life in the opposite direction to what you desire. Watch them as they turn to ashes. Observe the fire as they burn. Thank the fire for eliminating them from your life. If you don't want to burn them, you can tear the sheet of paper into shreds and flush the pieces down the toilet. Say goodbye to them. Appreciate the water that is taking them away.

Now, your new regulations are up-to-date. The ancestors are rejoicing. Thank them and celebrate. Put on some music and dance!

Assume Your Guilt over Being Different

One of the prices you had to pay for your healing was breaking your family rules. The next price you pay for healing is guilt. When you follow the rules in your group, you feel good and innocent; when you break them, you feel bad and guilty. To grow, you need to lose your innocence. What do you prefer—to feel innocent and stay small, or to feel some guilt and grow?

Do You Prefer to Preserve Your Innocence?

Matías is born into a family of lawbreakers. His father makes money by selling stolen property, and all the others in the family are in charge of collecting the merchandise. Ever since he was little, he has been trained in the art of stealing wallets from handbags and distracting people so that the adults in the family can similarly assault the victims. When things go "right"—that is to say, when they manage to steal a goodly amount because of his contribution—he feels good and innocent. His family is proud of him. "He's going to make a great thief!"

Matías grows up and falls in love with Blanca, who comes from a hardworking, honest family. In her family, stealing is considered wrong. Matías wants to marry Blanca and create a family of his own with her. In order for this to happen, he needs to be accepted by Blanca's family, and therefore he cannot carry on stealing. He gets a job working in a factory and studies at night. Blanca is very proud of him, but his family of origin feels let down. They think he's wasting his potential and could earn much more as a criminal. Matías has to choose between disappointing his family of origin and feeling guilty, or preserving his innocence.

People who prefer to preserve their innocence believe they cannot change. For example, Manuel thinks he's lazy and has no discipline. Every challenge is a huge hurdle for him, and he can barely manage to do what he sets out to do. He'd like to have the strength of will to do what he needs to do—from getting up early, eating healthy food, and exercising to no longer watching television at night. But his exhaustion is stronger than he is, and it overwhelms him. How often have you had something like this happen to you?

Preserving innocence gives you a sensation of tranquility. You believe you are being loyal to your family. In the beginning, you're loyal out of blind love for your family of origin. Later on, as you progress in life, you continue to reinforce these beliefs by surrounding yourself with people who act the same way—for example, Manuel's friends, who do exactly as he does.

When the people around you think that you are a certain way, it is more difficult for you to change because you have to go against the beliefs of the group you belong to, in addition to those of your family. Generally, the message that your group sends is: "With a lot of effort, you can make a few and small changes in the way you are or behave. But this only happens in a long and difficult process, with many stumbles. That's life, right?" No! Life is not like that. These are limiting beliefs that prevent you from growing and advancing. You have to break them as the price of feeling guilty. Or do you prefer to keep your innocence and get stuck?

The tranquility provided by being innocent is certainly a great temptation, but it leads you to believe that you can't change—that you are what your family taught you and what everyone thinks of you. This is why, believe it or not, most people prefer it this way. The price for growing up is too high, they believe, and many choose not to pay it.

But I believe you're ready to take a great leap forward in your evolution. You want to change and are willing to drop your innocence. True? Okay! Let's go!

Systemic Guilt

A system is a group of people united by certain beliefs and rules. A group can be a family, the members of a club, the inhabitants of a country, the congregation at a church, a social organization, the people working in a company, etc. Every system has an invisible legacy; that is what unites all its members. The group's entire history is stored in this legacy, what has happened to each member, and what is "good" or "bad" for the system.

The invisible legacy marks the limits that separate your system from other systems, clearly pointing out what it believes is right for the group and what is not. When a group runs the risk of disappearing as a result of various factors, its limits can become quite constricting. The more constricting the limits of a group, the stricter the rules become, and in order to do anything at all, it is often necessary to break those rules. The invisible legacy keeps you separated from anything that is different from your group with the hope of leading you down the "right path" and doing what is "right" by the group. How is this achieved? Through the sensation of systemic guilt.

For example, Marcela comes from a traditional family. Her father supported the household, and her mother took care of her. The rule in her family of origin is that the mother must stop working in order to raise the children. In her family, it is considered of vital importance to be present during the first years of the child's life. The mother might work, the rule goes, but only while her children are in school. Her professional activities have to come after tending to her husband and her children.

However, Marcela and her partner are from a different generation that has different beliefs. This generation believes that both parents should work and share the responsibility for raising children and supporting the family. To further reinforce these beliefs, Marcela sees her friends send their children to a nursery from early on, as they considered it important for women to have professional goals and aspirations. For this generation, being a housewife is not enough.

So now Marcela finds herself in a dilemma, and she doesn't know what to do. Her confusion is so great that she postpones getting married to her partner and having children. Guilt is eating her up. If she works, she'll be failing her children and her parents, and if she does not work, she'll be failing her children and her friends. No matter what she does, she believes she will have failed someone, so it's best not to have children.

This is happening to a lot of young adults nowadays; they are stuck in the middle of an internal battle of systemic rules that clash. When you discover something about yourself that is not in accordance with your system, you reject it, even if it's valuable to you. Marcela can't decide what would make her happy because of the guilt that, sadly, disconnects her from what she wants. The sound of the voices in the system you belong to can be so loud you can't hear your own voice. Only by getting those voices to be quiet will you be able to listen to your deepest yearnings.

Guilt is a plague preventing you from thriving when it permeates your life. Your decisions are paralyzed during this time of confusion. There's even a name for this phenomenon: *analysis paralysis*. You're paralyzed by your analysis of your options, since you're so afraid of making a mistake.

Guilt engulfs your life when you believe you've made a mistake. It's so unpleasant that you may possibly panic and block yourself from doing anything in an effort to avoid failing again. The good thing is that there is a solution for everything ... even guilt.

How to Stop Feeling Guilty

Not all guilt is the same. There are three types: real guilt, neurotic guilt, and systemic guilt. Every type of guilt has its remedy. Find the one you are experiencing, and you'll be able to heal yourself.

Real Guilt

Real guilt happens when you hurt someone and feel responsible for what you did. This type of guilt is appropriate and healthy and can help you offer the person you have hurt some form of compensation by doing something positive. If this guilt did not exist, people would go around in the world hurting each other without learning their lessons.

When you've hurt someone and are a conscious person, you feel bad and want to make amends. You also apologize, and the affected party receives your apology. Only when you have acknowledged your mistake will you stop repeating it; and, when you compensate for it, your guilt will dissipate.

Neurotic Guilt

Neurotic guilt is a sensation of anxiety and discomfort that covers over a real emotion: for example, repressed anger, denied fear, and sadness that has been stored for years. Neurotic guilt leads nowhere, and with it you cannot grow or take on responsibility. The only thing you can do is to go in deeper, walk through it, and dig out the real emotion.

Real emotions are not a problem when you feel and accept them, for they only last a few minutes. They will uncover unexpressed needs and then dilute them. Essentially, they'll evaporate. The problem you have with your emotions is that you cover them over and don't express them, and you prevent them from taking their natural course and disappearing.

Why do you cover over a real emotion with neurotic guilt? Because the real emotion you feel is prohibited in your family. If you were to allow yourself to feel it and accept it, you'd be the "bad guy" and would be plagued by systemic guilt. As you will see, systemic guilt is the worst of all!

Systemic Guilt

What emotion is prohibited in your family? In mine, it was fear—maybe because fear paralyzes, and with all the danger my ancestors lived through, the worst thing you could do was become paralyzed. This emotion was forbidden for a good reason, but that reason is no longer valid. The information has to be updated for it to be useful. Which emotion do you think is your forbidden one?

With systemic guilt, the feeling is so unpleasant, many people cover their real emotion with some other emotion that is permitted in the family—perhaps an emotion considered "good" for the system. In my family, joy is considered the best emotion. So when I'm afraid, my smile gets bigger, and the fear grows and grows; it's trying to alert me to something, but I'm not listening. Which emotion do you think might be the preferred one in your family? Very probably, that is the one you use to cover over your forbidden emotion.

Real emotions are important because they tell you what you need. Fear serves to protect you; anger is what you defend yourself with; and sadness helps you overcome your losses and rectify your path in life. If you aren't listening, you go through life without a compass and end up getting lost. But to be able to feel these emotions, you need to do things differently from the way they are done in your family system.

Systemic guilt is what you feel when you break the rules in your system, whether your family's or that of any group you belong to. Furthermore, you run the risk of being excluded and of no longer belonging to that group. As you know, the need to belong is most important to you, since it's terrifying to no longer belong to your group. It would be like being a balloon floating in the air with no direction.

Still, systemic guilt is the price you pay for growing. If you assume it, it'll dissipate over time. What happens in your growth process is the following: You have a limit you are familiar with, which is the farthest your tie of loyalty will allow you to go. Every time you stretch that tie, you're afraid of losing what you've known and will feel the guilt for doing things differently. If you can tolerate this sensation, you'll get used to it and stop experiencing it. Afterward, you'll be ready to stretch your cord even a little more, again feeling the guilt and fear, and if you can stand it like before, it'll dissolve again. This sense of guilt and of losing what you know and being excluded from your group is systemic guilt.

Your tie of loyalty is like the string that holds a helium-filled balloon. The balloon can fly freely, but if you release it, it will have no direction; without its string, the balloon gets lost in the sky. Yet if you simply lengthen the string a little, the balloon is capable of reaching even farther, and it can't get lost. Every balloon has a string that can be varied by different lengths, and it is this length that determines how high the balloon can fly.

Similarly, a person can lengthen ties of loyalty and fly very high, as high as he or she wishes, feeling free and happy and at the same time connected to and sustained by the groups to which he or she belongs. With the blessings of your ancestors, you are actively lengthening the ties of loyalty that bond you to your family and the groups you belong to. In this manner, you are still part of the group, but you grow. The price you pay for growing is the sensation of fear you feel when you move away from what you know and the guilt you feel over being different.

It's important to remember that in all systems, there will be people who prefer to preserve their innocence and who will not be able to tolerate the feeling of systemic guilt, even if it means they will be paying a bigger price to stay small and not change. These people will try to convince you to remain small with them by filling you with fear and guilt. It will be up to you to decide if you want to be swallowed up this way. All of us make choices according to the price we are willing to pay. All of us write our own destiny. What are you choosing for yours?

Accept Your Destiny and That of Everyone Else

Part of your destiny or your fate is already written because of the country you are born into, your family, and those life situations that somehow leave a mark on you. Nonetheless, you have a power within you that allows for any circumstance to be converted into an asset or a detriment to your good. What is this power that gets your life to change so radically? It's the power of free will.

When you learn to use this power correctly, you modify your life circumstances and rewrite your destiny. You've already done this without realizing it; you just need to keep doing what you've learned. Throughout this book, you've used your power for healing your family with the five keys. You've included all the members of your family. You have put things in order so that each can take up his or her own place and perform his or her function. You've taken life energy from your ancestors, balanced what you give and what you take in your relationships, and resolved the cycles of violence. All this you have achieved using the power of your free will. Bravo!

You've also learned to pay the price for healing by breaking the family rules and assuming the guilt over being different. The next price to pay for healing is accepting your destiny and that of everyone else. This is paradoxical, but only when you accept it will you be able to transform it.

The first step in resolving a problem is accepting that it exists. Well, it works the same with destiny: you accept what has been written in your destiny and can then rewrite it. First you must accept your life just as it is, acknowledging the way you live, the things that happen to you, what you like, and what you don't like. When you stop fighting and resisting your destiny, you'll be able to make changes when the time comes to make choices.

What do I mean by that? There are things in your destiny that you do not choose, and there are things that you do. You can make changes when it's time to make a decision. These moments are known as *choice points*, and some of them are *Y points or forks in the road that change your direction.*

I could write an entire book on this subject, as I find it fascinating, but for the moment you only need the basics. There are some things that happen in your life that you didn't choose, and this is just the way things are. These you accept, and in doing so, you avoid wasting your energy getting into a rage over trying to change them or feeling sorry for what has happened to you. On the other hand, there are things you face that come with an option—something you will need to choose between. This is where your attention needs to be focused. Some of these choice points become Y points because they are decisions that leave a mark on your life.

Every day offers hundreds of choice points, and all of a sudden one of them—though it might seem small to you, almost insignificant—becomes in reality a Y point. Surprise! Your life will shift because of that decision. I'm sure that if you try, you'll recall some small decision you made that got your life to shift in a different direction.

There are decisions you already know as Y points. For example, a career, moving to another country, getting married, having children—these are big decisions that imply life changes. But there are many other decisions that appear to be really small, such as going to a party; yielding your seat on an airplane and arriving at your destination hours later; or accompanying a friend to have lab tests done. These appear to be everyday decisions, but what would happen if at the party you were to meet someone who leaves a mark on your life (a mate, the partner with whom you'll build a successful company, etc.), or if the plane you decided not to board crashed, or if by accompanying your friend to have the tests done you discovered you have an injury and are now just in time to have it tended to, saving your life. These are choice points that turn into Y points.

When you do not accept your destiny or that of another person, you feel angry, sad, or afraid. You block the wisdom in your system. You're focused on changing what is happening, but you do not have the power with which to do that. Your attention is placed on struggling, and when the choice points arrive, you're moving in a direction opposite to what you desire. In the process, you miss out on the opportunities that present themselves for you to rewrite your destiny. This you do because the emotions you are feeling cloud your judgment, and they don't allow you to see the right path.

If you accept your destiny and that of others, you face your choice points from a centered place and have access to the wisdom in your family system. You use your power of choice freely and do so with the help of your ancestors. Your ancestors accompany you and keep you on the alert—centered, relaxed, and happy. Accept what is, and every day will be better.

Find Wiser Solutions

You've paid the final price for healing, and now you have access to wiser solutions. Where are the wiser solutions to be found? With your ancestors? Ancestors have many solutions, but the wisest are to be found in something greater still: the source of life. People have different beliefs about this, so adapt this explanation to what makes sense to your unique way of understanding it.

The source of life is the place from which the substance that animates everything arises. If human beings were water, the waterfall from which all sprouted would be the source of life. All the wisest solutions are to be found there. And how can you reach this source of life? As you undertake this healing, you connect to life and flow with it. As you feel life, take life, and give life, you are one with it. Then you and the source of life are no longer separate; you are one.

It sounds very poetic, and you might wish for a more complete explanation, but this can only be learned through experience. In time, you'll understand. You just have to do your part, and the solutions will find you.

Apply the Magui Block Method to Pay the Price of Healing and Liberate Yourself

You've reached the last part of the book. There are many reasons for you to feel proud of yourself, for only a particular group will choose to accomplish this. I congratulate you! The benefits will be incredible, and you'll reap the harvest during the coming months.

Using the following statements, you will ground the work you have done and transform yourself as if by magic. The results will be extraordinary!

Start by adopting the right physical posture, as follows:

- Hold your body upright. Imagine that your head is touching the sky and that your feet are firmly and deeply grounded in the earth.

- Be centered. Your heart and mind are as clear as crystal.

- Place your hands, one over the other, on your belly button. Imagine that they connect to the space that is close to your spine, inside of your body. (If you're a woman, place the palm of your right hand on your belly button and the palm of the left hand on the back of your right hand. If you're a man, place the palm of your left hand on your belly button and the palm of the right hand on the back of your left hand.)

Next, evoke love:

- Remember your willingness to heal, and smile.

- Feel appreciation for yourself.

- Be thankful for the moment.

Finally, appreciate the power of these words :

- Repeat these phrases out loud.

- Listen to the way you say them, and repeat them until they come naturally to you.

Now, adopt the right posture, evoke love, and repeat the following out loud:

> *I've paid the price of healing.*
> *I've burned my family's rules, the ones that were blocking my way to being who I am and doing what benefits me.*
> *I've transformed my family loyalties so they now propel me lovingly toward my goals.*
> *I've created my personal set of regulations with rules that guide me to fulfill my potential.*
> *I now put into practice what I have learned.*
> *I assume the guilt over being different from my family.*
> *I assume the guilt over being different from the other systems I belong to.*
> *I've paid the price of healing.*
> *I drop the innocence and I grow.*
> *I assume the systemic guilt, and it dilutes quickly.*
> *I am increasingly free and happy.*
> *I liberate myself from guilt and live a full life.*
> *I've paid the price of healing.*
> *I express my real emotions.*
> *I accept my destiny, and I rewrite it.*
> *I accept each person's destiny and respect each person's free will.*
> *I use the power of my choices wisely.*
> *I've paid the price of healing.*
> *My ancestors guide me.*
> *I connect to the source of life, and the wisest solutions come to me.*

I accept my destiny, and I rewrite it.
I accept each person's destiny and respect each person's
*   free will.*
I use the power of my choice wisely.
I've paid the price of healing.
My ancestors guide me.
I connect to the source of life.
The wisest solutions come to me.
My family has healed.
My family has healed.
My family has healed.
Thank you.

And you and your ancestors celebrate in joy!

About the Author

M AGUI BLOCK RECEIVED A BACHELOR'S degree in administration. During her work as an administrator and consultant, she developed an interest in understanding human beings and the dynamics of interpersonal relationships. This is how she started working with psychotherapy more than twenty-five years ago, studying various specializations and finally creating her own method for achieving extraordinary results in very little time. Currently, she offers diplomas for training professional facilitators in the Magui Block Method, besides offering consultations and continually creating tools for transforming through love. *Check out her website at* www.maguiblock.com.

Glossary

Blind love: The feeling that gets all the members of a system (family or group) to sacrifice themselves for one another. This sacrifice can take place in many ways; for example, by repeating a tragic story, carrying a disease, having an accident, or giving up on your dreams to satisfy those of someone else.

Emotional Freedom Technique (EFT): An exercise combining elements of psychology and acupuncture. It is a technique in which the human energy system is stimulated by tapping to produce emotional balance. It consists of softly tapping with the fingertips on some energy meridian points on the body five or seven times as you create a "target." A target is thinking and/or expressing out loud what you wish to dissolve or integrate. This exercise is very effective when the target is correctly chosen.

Eye Movement Desensitization and Reprocessing (EMDR): There is a natural eye movement that occurs every night during sleep that helps you digest and integrate what you have experienced in the course of the day. When traumatic events occur, this movement becomes insufficient, and some issues are left pending resolution. By moving your eyes in a conscious manner with the intention of processing all that is still pending, you can help retrieve what is missing. This is a very effective psychotherapy technique that was created by Francine Shapiro.

Family patterns: Thoughts, feelings, and behavior—repetitive and automatic—that you inherit from your family system.

Family Constellations: A type of systemic family psychotherapy developed by Bert Hellinger, who says that 80 percent of the psychological problems that affect people come from their family history and relationships. Family Constellations sheds light on the dynamics that cause suffering and, if this occurs under the appropriate circumstances, corrects them in that instant.

Family system: The set of persons, alive or dead, who share the invisible family legacy.

Honoring: Respecting someone; treating a person with dignity.

Internal images: Mental representations. They can show the shape the family system is in. By ordering them, you transform your life and heal.

Invisible family legacy: Everything you receive from your family system; the information that comes in your mother's egg and your father's sperm. It includes what you receive at the unconscious level from your biological family—not only what happened in the past but also what is still occurring in the present.

Perpetrator: A person, force, or energy that harms another. This damage can be caused intentionally or unintentionally. The damage can be physical, material, moral, or psychological. Perpetrators are those who steal, attack, commit crimes, are aggressive, take part in terrorist acts, kill, hurt another in an accident, etc.

System: A group of people united by certain beliefs and rules. A group can be a family, the members of a club, the inhabitants of a country, the members of a religion or a social organization, those who work in a company, etc. Every system has an invisible legacy, which unites all its members.

Systemic tugs: Sensations and perceptions that get you to do things without your realizing it, out of blind love, by sacrificing yourself and repeating the stories of the members in your system. Systemic tugs are like the currents in the sea; they tug at you in a direction you do not wish to go.

Taking: Accepting others as they are, without conditions. When you are taking from others, you open up and receive everything that comes to you from them.

Tapas Acupressure Technique (TAT): An exercise created by acupuncturist Tapas Fleming for resolving allergic and emotional problems. It is an easy technique to apply, and the manual can be downloaded free of charge from the following website: www.tatlife.com.

Victim: One who suffers from damage provoked by one or several persons, or by overwhelming forces, such as natural disasters or wars. A victim not only feels powerless but is so in reality. A victim feels panic, is overwhelmed by circumstances, and depends completely on help provided by another. Victims are those who suffer from things like medical malpractice, theft, kidnapping, murder, rape, attacks, accidents, terrorism, wars, and losses due to natural disasters.

Wise love: The most elevated feeling there is. It helps you transform family patterns and feel profound respect for the destiny of each member in your system (family or group). When you feel it, you stop sacrificing yourself and find wiser solutions.

Bibliography

Hellinger, Bert. 2006. *Después del conflicto, la paz.* Argentina. Editorial Alma Lepik.

Hellinger, Bert. 2006. *Los órdenes de la ayuda.* Argentina. Editorial Alma Lepik.

Hellinger, Bert. 2002. *El centro se distingue por su levedad.* Conferencias e historias terapéuticas. Spain. Editorial Herder.

Hellinger, Bert. 2006. *La paz inicia en el alma.* Mexico. Editorial Herder.

Weber, Gunthard, ed. 2001. *Felicidad Dual. Bert Hellinger y su psicoterapia sistémica.* Spain. Editorial Herder.

Hellinger, Bert. 2001. *Religión, Psicoterapia, Cura de almas.* Textos recopilados. Spain. Editorial Herder.

Hellinger, Bert. 2001. *Órdenes del Amor. Cursos seleccionados de Bert Hellinger.* Spain. Editorial Herder.

Hellinger, Bert y Ten Hôvel Gabriele. 2001. *Reconocer lo que es. Conversaciones sobre implicaciones y desenlaces logrados.* Spain. Editorial Herder.

Neuhauser, Johannes, ed. 2001. *Lograr el amor en la pareja. El trabajo de Bert Hellinger con parejas.* Spain. Editorial Herder.

Hellinger, Bert y Bolzmann, Tiju, 2003. *"Imágenes que solucionan"* en el Taller de Constelaciones Familiares. Trabajo Terapéutico Sistémico. Argentina. Editorial Alma Lepik.

Printed in the United States
By Bookmasters